What in the World Is Going On?

Wisdom Teachings for Our Time

Penny Gill

in Conversation with Tibetan Teacher Manjushri

for Lehua,

with all good wishes!

Penny Gill

BALBOA
PRESS

A DIVISION OF HAY HOUSE

Balboa Press books may be ordered through booksellers or by contacting:

Balboa Press
A Division of Hay House
1663 Liberty Drive
Bloomington, IN 47403
www.balboapress.com
1 (877) 407-4847

Because of the dynamic nature of the Internet, any web addresses or links contained in this book may have changed since publication and may no longer be valid. The views expressed in this work are solely those of the author and do not necessarily reflect the views of the publisher, and the publisher hereby disclaims any responsibility for them.

The author of this book does not dispense medical advice or prescribe the use of any technique as a form of treatment for physical, emotional, or medical problems without the advice of a physician, either directly or indirectly. The intent of the author is only to offer information of a general nature to help you in your quest for emotional and spiritual well-being. In the event you use any of the information in this book for yourself, which is your constitutional right, the author and the publisher assume no responsibility for your actions.

Any people depicted in stock imagery provided by Thinkstock are models, and such images are being used for illustrative purposes only.
Certain stock imagery © Thinkstock.

Printed in the United States of America.

ISBN: 978-1-5043-2611-7 (sc)
ISBN: 978-1-5043-2612-4 (e)

Balboa Press rev. date: 1/19/2014

Informed by a lifetime of teaching, academic disciplinary scholarship, and an immersion in Eastern and Western reflective practices and spiritual traditions, Penny Gill's book is a deeply transformative, utterly radical and ultimately optimistic reframing of the seemingly insurmountable challenges facing our civilization and our species. Wise, analytic, and disciplined, the beautiful narrative explores the principles of interconnectedness and fearfulness, achieving profound insights and comprising nothing less than a new secular gospel for our times.

Donal O'Shea, President, New College of Florida, Professor of
Mathematics, and author of "The Poincare Conjecture"

Fascinating, mysterious, and wise, Penny Gill's book is a Platonic dialogue for what she terms the "post-religion, post-ethics, and post-materialism" age. The Buddha-like Teacher describes the deep structure and meaning of the cosmos and the evolution of consciousness, of mind knowing Mind.

Recognizing their shared consciousness, human beings can find like-minded souls and move beyond the dark obsessions and tyrannies of modern life. This is ultimately a positive book, a celebration of the transformative potential of Cosmic Mind.

Joanne V. Creighton, President Emerita, Mount Holyoke
College, Five College Professor of English

A marvel of long listening and patient receptivity, this book flings open windows to the worlds beyond our own.

Christian McEwen, author of "World Enough and Time: On Creativity and Slowing
Down" and "Sparks from the Anvil: the Smith College Poetry Interviews"

... an extraordinarily valuable, immediately useful, and surprisingly hopeful perspective on the human, environmental, and cosmic world. It resonates with the most enlightened writings by philosophers, scientists, and mystics, and points the way to skillful action necessary to avert the worst effects of the global crises we humans have unleashed.

Randy Kehler: peace and social justice activist and founder
of the Promoting Active Nonviolence project.

For all who hold the world in their hearts.

Deep is calling unto deep.
—Psalm 42

Nothing is solid. Proceed as if in a dream.
—Kwan Yin

Contents

Preface

Before going to bed last night, I went out on the deck, as I always do. I lingered while my eyes adjusted to the deep darkness. As the sky slowly filled with stars over the vast expanse of Lake Superior, I stretched out on the chaise; wordless, nearly breathless from the beauty, I soaked in its immensity. Each star pulsing with energy is a giant sun, and our galaxy, whose edge I could see faintly overhead, only one of countless others.

What do the teachings mean? I wondered. A lovely story created by generations of Himalayan people to help them live well and learn to be kind to one another? And what more do we really need?

There is so little we really know. Who can grasp even a fraction of the reality I swam in last night? Or of the miracle that I am here to witness it? Can a puny human brain leap into that expanse? Can human concepts grasp its depth? Can we really understand our place in the cosmos?

I imagined the great Buddhist deities of compassion and wisdom, Kwan Yin and Manjushri, flowing out into that huge sky, until each was a harmonic pulse, an energy pattern. How then could that shape-shift into some form able to communicate? And why would it want to?

I don't know how to answer those questions, because any answer requires more assumptions than I am comfortable with. I prefer to hold the tension between that limitless night sky and my little mind.

May these teachings challenge, comfort, and inspire you, cherished fellow student. And together, may we lighten the suffering of all beings.

Madeline Island
LaPointe, Wisconsin
July, 2014

| First Mapping

So, Miss Penny-la (a dark, low, unmistakably older male voice and presence says). The first thing we want you to understand much more fully is the state of your world, what is really happening there, how to "read" the current situation, and how to understand it in a much wider developmental context. To do this completely is a huge task. You may choose whether you'd like a very brief summary now or a much more developed account over days, perhaps a week or two.

Oh, sir, I'd like the fullest account I can have. You know, I've been interested in that broad question all my life. I have plenty of time, especially if we can do this in small, daily installments.

Okay. Then we will begin. Later, then, my colleagues will teach you about some other topics: consciousness and the mind, freedom and human responsibility, the possibilities of language, and much more. But let us begin.

First, let's be clear. This will become an extensive set of teachings, a well-developed way of understanding the human world and the trajectory of human life and consciousness. We don't want you dithering about what you are to do with this. Obviously, it's not only for you. It may well develop so fully that it can be a book—either our book, a book received from "the other side," with all that implies, or your book, with our participation muted and disguised. That has its own advantages, as we know. My point is this: Recognize we are beginning a big project that is not only for you personally. Agree that its ultimate voice and form can be decided later. Free yourself from those concerns, or it will inhibit the flow of information. And we'd suggest you experiment with writing directly on the computer, which would be much easier for you.

Okay, sir. I am ready on the computer. It would be very good indeed if this would work.

You see the world from several perspectives: you see states and global forces such as markets and how they shape the parameters within which people live. You also have a strong focus on individuals, how they find meaning, how they proceed with their lives, and how they meet their most essential psychosocial and spiritual needs. You have often found the tension between these two views, which you describe as political and spiritual, to be very difficult to handle. You have done some of your most creative teaching and thinking by trying to be in the space between and around them. It has stimulated some of your best work with students because you have never lost sight of their deeper personal issues. And it has given you a perpetual sense of not being a legitimate academic, not quite belonging to that world. That has been a source of unease for you. Eventually, through our work together, these two viewpoints will be much better integrated, largely by expanding the framework of your thinking. The core question, which has so dogged you all your life, is what is the purpose and meaning of human life? We will try to shape a viable answer for you. No, not right. There *is* an answer, and we will try to teach you enough so that you can understand it.

This is a story about the evolution of humans, which has not been primarily driven by the pressures of adapting to the local environment but by the pressures of responding to ever-increasing needs to relate to Spirit. That is a big claim, and it will take some time for us to explain to you what that means and how it has happened. It is not that suddenly Darwin's scheme is no longer operative for humans. In fact, it certainly is operative on the level of DNA and organic functioning. But human life, as it is of interest to us now, has been relatively brief, too brief for much change on a physical level. Most adaptations to the shifting environment have been behavioral and cultural, and the knowledge of what works best is stored culturally as best practices and traditions. No need to discuss that now. The point is that that is what governs human development as seen within the concrete, embodied physical environment.

But that is only one environment within which humans live. They also live within the environment of Spirit, the invisible world that permeates and surrounds all human life. All life, in fact. This has not been as well studied and understood by contemporary humans, certainly not in the West. It is time now for you to understand this equally significant process. Unless you recognize its centrality, there is no possibility of making the right decisions or the right interventions to shape humanity's future.

This will be our project: To truly understand the world right now, you must understand human life and activity from the point of view of Spirit and of human life within its context of Spirit (those are not the same). Humans, like all organisms, respond skillfully or unskillfully to major changes in their environment. The skillful species survive; the unskillful species disappear. Humanity has arrived at such a moment. You consider global warming, climate change, and environmental degradation as the major change in the human environment, and indeed, those are very important. But far more important and far more impactful are the shifts in the environment of Spirit, in the impulses and processes and energies generated by Spirit and which encase all human life. Indeed, all earthly life. Global warming, in this view, is a metaphor for other more significant challenges. We can use Darwin's basic idea and ask if humans have the capacity to respond to great shifts in their physical environment within which they produce and reproduce. We can ask if humans have the commitment (we know they have the capacity) to respond to the new pressures arising from the realm of Spirit. Keep that question in the back of your mind as we proceed these next weeks and months.

Here are topics we will discuss with you:

1) Humans do indeed live in an environment of Spirit, which has its own trajectory and significance.
2) Much of what is difficult to understand in the human world today, especially the level of violence and suffering, is better understood through the dimension of Spirit.
3) Globalization and all it implies offers both crisis and opportunity unparalleled in human history.
4) Traditional religious traditions and teachings are not muscular enough to respond to these challenges, especially given the habit of looking backward for solutions. The era of the "great teacher" is over, which has many implications for human education and culture.
5) Consciousness is the key to understand this and the instrument to address it. Human life must turn to a new and potent focus on

3

increasing consciousness in every sector of human society, but most especially in education, health care, environmental policy, and the uses of power and authority.

6) For consciousness to flourish, freedom is essential—a freedom embedded in the practices of compassion and wisdom.

This briefly outlines the book and gives you a glimpse of the shape of the argument. It is, as we said, very big. And there is, as you have said, plenty of time. Let me assure you, this will be the most exciting and satisfying thing you have ever done in your life. (It is excellent that you can do this so easily on the computer. It will make this much easier.) This is all for today. We will continue tomorrow. As we proceed, we will develop our own rhythm and pace. Think now that we will spend about an hour each morning doing this.

The Teacher Introduces Himself

Good morning, sir. It seems I must open our session. Is that true? And what shall I call you when I speak to or about you?

Yes, you sensed my presence as I came into focus. Your addressing me opens the channel and indicates your willingness to participate. We *never* do this without the full assent of our human partner. This is very important for you to understand. So, yes, my energy, the energy that I am, will then be present and come into focus, and then you must initiate the conversation.

What shall you call me? I notice you do not ask who I am, perhaps out of respect and perhaps mixed with a little fear or trepidation. I am a being you have not encountered before, though I have been paying attention to you for some time. Kwan Yin has been our "face" with you, as she has brought you to this level of maturity and clarity. We work together, cooperating in our desire to increase the level of consciousness among human beings. She heals, supports, and prepares the containers; my energy pours in then, when it can be best received. It is a very good partnership. You could say I am her male consort, and that as she embodies compassion, I embody wisdom. Her purpose is healing, and my purpose is opening awareness; of course you are now beginning to understand those are two aspects of a single process of maturation, and there is no difference between us. The Tibetans call this aspect *Manjushri*, and that is how they recognize me. They are devoted to the pursuit of this wisdom, and I care for them and teach them. I will do the same with you, if you choose to develop your devotion to this work.

This project will recast your understanding of wisdom. In many ways, you have been a wise person and have been recognized as such by those around you. Yours is a wisdom about human relationships and human life, about how to shape a life, and the need for profound meaning. This is very valuable, and in fact, human societies are held together by those who have learned and shared this wisdom. This is a feeling-based wisdom, as it lives in and concerns itself with the human heart.

The wisdom we will introduce you to is of a different realm. This is not a wisdom about the human heart but rather about the deep structure and meaning of the cosmos. The teaching is about mind, consciousness, and the evolution of consciousness within the cosmos. It will teach you about the earth and the human world, but its point of view will not be grounded in the details of human life. To safely learn of this level of wisdom or to receive this kind of teaching, a human being must be deeply knowledgeable about human life. Otherwise, there is a risk either of foolishness—not grasping the implications of what we teach—or of losing one's groundedness in human reality. I speak there not of psychiatric disturbance, for there is no danger of that with you, but of swinging out into a realm of speculation, where you might find quite a bit of surprising company! (He laughs.) Later on you will be surprised to see how certain patterns repeat on multiple levels, the microcosm reflecting the macrocosm. This is what allows for interpretation. You will also see how shifting the context also shifts your understanding of what is actually happening in any particular event.

Though we speak to you of two levels or realms of wisdom, the purpose of this project is to lay out the relationship between them. In other words, the reason for teaching you the larger cosmic view of the current situation is that some very specific human responses are called for now. So we will look at implications and consequences, paying attention to both the macro and the micro levels. By micro, I mean human life in its complex social and political organizations. Individual human life is even more micro; perhaps we should call it nano life? (We both laugh. He wants me to know how well informed he is about life on earth!) The macro level is the cosmic, the widest possible view.

I introduced the concept yesterday of the double evolutionary paths of human beings, one the organic or physiological, and the other spiritual consciousness or relationship with Spirit or Mind. Although the former actually brought human beings into existence as a life form, it has had very little to do with the evolution of consciousness or the human relationship to Spirit. One reason is that there simply hasn't been enough time for this to be found at a genetic level. Perhaps some day. The vehicle now and for a very long time has been reincarnation, which allows for the accumulation of experience and knowledge of Spirit from one life to another. The other vehicle has been culture, by which various understandings and practices are passed on as an inheritance to the next generation of seekers.

Neither of these vehicles is adequate anymore. More substantial and rapid change is required now, and it must include a radical transformation of human self-understanding. This is in fact underway, and you are certainly part of that, as are many of your friends and colleagues. Ancient Buddhists spoke of *kalpas*, an unimaginably long period of earthly time during which one would experience every possible life form. This has its own fundamental mythic truth. But now humans are developing very sophisticated theories about the origins of the visible universe and its most basic physical properties and processes. This is very exciting and a real tribute to human inventiveness and intellectual brilliance. Now you know the universe is expanding, that the energy released in the first few seconds is still driving the expansion, and that human beings are made of the chemicals organized in those first chemical reactions billions and billions of years ago.

Still, astrophysicists and cosmologists think day and night about all they do not know: What started this extraordinary process? What are black holes and dark matter? What is light?

We share with humans our puzzlement about the cosmos, and like you, we wonder why it is, rather than is not. There is no being who knows the answer. By the way, one convenient way to assess the consciousness of beings is to consider who asks that question and who does not.

We also know cycles are not the fundamental patterns of motion in the cosmos, as many ancient traditions have believed. Rather, the universe is expanding; energy is pulsing, released from its original center into all directions, if one can even speak of directions. Every sentient being is a miniature receiver and transformer of energy, with built-in receptors for various kinds and frequencies of energy. Each being has a range of possibilities for transforming and in turn sending out energy at various frequencies. What you call life is actually these interlocking systems of receiving, transforming, and sending out energy. Much mental life is a dimension of those energetic processes.

We often speak of Spirit and of human relationships with Spirit, as if it were a subject/object relationship. It is not, of course. Humans do not exist outside of Spirit. Human life is embodied Spirit. Those whose "spiritedness" is undernourished or blocked do not flourish. So even though we will speak often of how to shift the human understanding of and relationship with Spirit, we are actually always referring to the many processes of becoming more aware of what already is true. This is where the two great issues come together; deepening the human relationship to Spirit is not the critical piece. What is critical is the compelling necessity for humans to be aware of Spirit and their relationship to Spirit; in fact, humans must recognize their own life in Spirit and of their own identity as Spirit. Every being is reminded on the way to its next life: "Remember, you are Spirit." None ever does. The forces of forgetting and unconsciousness are simply overwhelming.

So what is Spirit? What is mind? What is consciousness? By the end of this extended teaching, you should understand this much better. Right now, remember Spirit is energy, energy not visible to the human eye, though it can make itself visible through its consequences. When we say Spirit's energy is not visible, we mean it works at frequencies that cannot be seen by human eyes. It cannot be seen or heard or sensed in the usual ways. Think of Spirit as a band of invisible frequencies that cannot be detected through the five senses of humans or the machines that amplify those senses. (*I keep thinking of black holes and dark matter.*) Yes. Those are powerhouses of Spirit energy pulsing out into the cosmos.

What distinguishes Spirit energy is that it can express intention. That will turn out to be highly significant, so write that again: Spirit energy can express intention, unlike most other forms and frequencies of energy. In fact, Spirit is pure intention. Whose, you might ask? Intention of what? The answer is Mind. Spirit expresses the intention of cosmic Mind. And Mind must know itself. That is what we call consciousness. Mind knowing itself is the intention, the purpose, the point, and perhaps the meaning of it all.

Then you ask, for you ask excellent questions, what is the relationship between Mind and this energetic realm we call the cosmos? What does this have to do with little human life down on earth? There we must stop, because you are very tired.

7

I bow to you in deep gratitude, great Manjushri. I do not understand much of what you have said today. It is too vast and abstract for me to grasp now.

This is an introduction and a first mapping to help you get some sense of language and scope. We are learning how to proceed with you. Each student is different. You seem to want more order and more full development of a point. We will find our best way to work together. Trust that, please. This has been a good session. Rest now.

The Shower of Spirit

Good morning, illustrious sir.

Please do not be spooked by all of this. Let me reiterate what Kwan Yin has taught you, that this project is for the good and well-being of others. You have long recognized your world needed to exercise more compassion. That cannot happen until your world receives more wisdom about what the real situation is, how things are shifting, and which energies are moving human society and human possibilities and in which ways. People desperately need, and know they need, this big picture, this new way of framing many pressing old issues. Your availability to us is your gift to your world. You are a teacher in every bone of your body. This will be the teaching of your lifetime, and truly, it will give you great joy and satisfaction. Please take this in. It is very important that you be relaxed and comfortable and willing to be available. Perhaps this will help you understand more fully your part in this larger process.

What is the condition of the world and the world's peoples this teaching will address? There is much to say. We will do a first sketch this morning, as we have done the previous mornings, a first mapping. Then we will develop the various lines of enquiry much more fully, one at a time. Your mind requires the overview first, so you can see how all the parts will fit together.

There are three interlocked, central phenomena right now that must be understood: population, environmental degradation, and conflict and violence. There are too many people on earth now, which accelerates the competition for resources and land. The result is unsustainable development and production and conflict over scarce resources. Although many current violent conflicts are wrapped in the language of identities and ideological goals, the truth is they arise out of deep fear of losing adequate access to the necessities of life—land, water, and natural resources—and rage over their inequitable and unjust distribution.

We don't disagree with your analysis; however, we see it from a different point of view. For example, we have watched an unprecedented number of souls racing to be born in these times. They wish to be present for the great transformation, and they wish to clear out eons of difficult karma. This level of global population is not biologically comprehensible; in other words, no species would allow this much overpopulation for any length of time. It is, in a strange way of speaking, an "unnatural" phenomenon. It will not last. From our side, the enthusiasm to be on earth is waning, and the pressures for clearing karma are diminishing. From the earthly side, there will be biological pressures that reduce population, including opportunistic factors arising from the intense overcrowding: epidemic disease, environmental collapse, and warfare. It is nearly impossible for humans to see this with any equanimity, but you could consider this a healing crisis for the planet as a whole. This is not a trajectory that will be followed out to "the edge of the graph." It is not sustainable. The current crisis point will lead to a sharp correction and a more sustainable equilibrium.

What is this "great transformation" that the souls wanted to participate in? In other words, what is the larger context of the problems as they present themselves to earthly thinkers? Many have spoken of this before. Because you and many of your future readers are ignorant of that, let me give a brief summary. One might consider this whole project to be a teaching about the changes originating in the realm of Spirit and their implications for humans.

Recall from yesterday that Mind wishes to know itself. Recent human history has been marked by intense social and economic development. Globalization is a recent flowering of this impulse: human exploration of their physical world, especially through science and technology, the development of new economic and political institutions, and a vigorous experiment releasing the powers of the autonomous individual. Much thoughtful and creative human energy has explored some aspect of what you now call modernity.

What has not received much energy or attention? The life of Spirit. The true life of the mind. The practices of meaning. The development of skillful means to open to Spirit, to clarify and expand consciousness, and to become inhabitants of the cosmos as well as of earth. This imbalance (quite an inadequate word, for we are describing a radical disequilibrium) is unmatched at any earlier period of human history. This cannot continue. When I say that, I do not mean we will not allow it to continue, or that any power greater than we are will interrupt it. I mean it cannot continue because its own internal pressures are undermining the very ground upon which it rests. It is, as you might say, an utterly natural occurrence, the consequence of its own decisions and values.

None of this is "bad," or should have been avoided. It is a necessary stage of human development, but it is only a stage. Now it is time (in fact, it is already well underway) for that total concentration on the visible, material dimensions of human life to give way to make room for new ways to recognize Spirit and its significance for human life. The "great transformation" that so many have spoken of in the past expresses some aspects of this: Spirit has traveled deeply into the human and material visible world, and now has begun her "return trip." Mind wishes to know itself. Spirit penetrated matter, creating countless life forms within which to express itself. Fully extended, she (or it, as you wish) has begun the return to self-consciousness. Spirit's intention is to bring with her as many of these life forms as she possibly can, for each is a moment of self-consciousness, of Mind knowing Mind.

This will not turn the world into a great contemplative monastery! There is a huge infusion of powerful spiritual energy—witness yourself, for example—and its intention is to be known by every available "knower." That is why so many crowded into earth these decades. Every soul wants to be available for this great showering of Spirit on this planet. You look around at your world and are flooded with grief. We look around it and see the shower of Spirit and are flooded with joy. We will explain this more fully in the next days and weeks, but this is the large outline of what you must understand and then teach. It reflects the essential "logic" of Spirit, and it does not depend on human virtue to continue. It is much vaster than that. Your task is to understand this large framing as fully as you can, and then to see what appropriate human responses might be.

The Great Transformation: An Introduction

We have briefly laid out for you the large picture. This is a time of profound transformation, and Earth is caught in its throes without having much understanding. This makes humans fall back into their familiar concepts of cause and effect: natural law, vice and virtue, good and evil, uncontrolled greed, and systems that escape human management. None of that is irrelevant, but neither is any of it causal. There is no question of blame here nor of some kind of autonomous evil.

This transformation has its origin in the cosmos, way beyond the ken of humans on earth. It impacts Earth via immaterial energy, with frequencies very different from those that materialize as form and shape in sentient beings or matter. Humans play an insignificantly tiny role in Earth's energy systems, and Earth similarly plays an insignificant role in the cosmic energy system.

One piece of this coming transformation is that humans must truly recognize the value of becoming cosmically and astronomically literate. There is a major energetic transformation underway within the cosmos, and it is beginning to impact earth and earthly life. Humans have no choice but to respond to it. The question is: What kind of response would be most appropriate and "cooperative" with the transformation underway? And that is the purpose of this project. We wish to lay out the situation to help all the students understand it deeply. Then we will situate the students so they can teach others. The more people who can grasp this reframed analysis of the troubles on earth, the easier and more likely that human responses can be appropriate and adequate.

Humans traditionally have described these moments of cosmic transformation in apocalyptic terms. Contemporary versions wrap it in narratives of invasions from outer space or planetary wars or the final judgment by an angry god. Human minds catch some aspects of this energetic valence, but their imaginations reduce it to such simple forms that the meaning is lost. Pity. Little boys love stories about asteroids striking earth, and many are fascinated with the dinosaurs and their sudden disappearance. But that too was a change initiated by new energy, in the form of matter arriving from outside the system.

This time it does not appear as matter. The energy has not materialized. It is subtle energy of a very high frequency, and very potent. It is setting the earth's energy at a different frequency, which in turn will affect the functioning of every being on the planet. Think of it this way: The earth is a singing bowl, and the regular flow of energy to and around it has kept it singing a nice steady pitch for millions of years. Now someone comes along and runs the stick around its edge. The pitch shifts as the bowl gains more and more energy. The volume increases. The harmonics stretch out further; there is more resonance and sympathetic vibration within and around the bowl. You can feel it with your hands if you come close. This is what is happening to Earth. New and stronger pulses of energy are arriving, and the earth responds; it can't help but respond. The frequencies are higher and stronger. There is much more resonance, more harmonic pulses are released, and even electromagnetic forces shift in response.

Since every being is its own self-contained energetic system (that is the fundamental definition of "being," after all), each is impacted in some way or another by the shift in the earth's energetic fields. As the bowl sings at a different pitch and with a different volume, the small bowls around it begin to vibrate differently. What are the implications for life on earth?

It is a huge question. We will start with a discussion of the several energy fields of every organism, something you and your culture are woefully ignorant of. We will show how they are interrelated and how they each affect functioning. This will help you understand how energy shifts arriving into the earth's system impact earthly beings. The revolution in consciousness—or in simple knowledge—happens when humans recognize that significant elements shaping human life on earth are not only material and human, but also non-material and non-human. Can humans learn these things without reverting to some pre-scientific, mythic narrative? The point of each life, of agreeing to be born in human form, after all, is to expand consciousness, not contract it to some earlier imagined indigenous lifestyle. Not only lifestyle, but also spiritual lifestyle.

The extraordinary attractiveness of indigenous practices and beliefs for people imprisoned in contemporary, materialist, secular life tells it all; people are desperate for better balance, and this will require some way to undermine the iron grip of materialism. They hurry to the only example they see—shamans and exorcisms and earth rituals. None of it is really harmful, and it does hold open a psychological space for new consciousness. However, it is a regressive movement, which often denies the complexities of contemporary science and consciousness.

Brief Summary

Good morning, sir. I apologize for my absence the last two days. I think the energy got too intense for me and I had to take a break.

No apology needed. It is very important that you know you can set the pace of our work here. It is not meant to go on in spite of your needs; it is meant to enrich and nourish your own growth and depth of understanding. No one can learn when under stress, so you were correct to pause and deal with your own stress this week. We've noticed that you also are finding this very cerebral and abstract, cognitive rather than heart-centered. This is a misunderstanding, and we will try to adjust that for you. It is certainly not our intention to lay down another barrier between your heart and mind.

Today I will introduce you to one more essential preliminary, and then we will have completed our first mapping and our introduction.

We have talked about humans as a species and how the species has developed. We have talked about shifts in the cosmic energy system and have offered a few sentences about mind, consciousness, and evolution. We've reported that many beings have come to earth at this moment because there is a great showering of Spirit upon earthly beings, the beginning of a great transformation. We've reminded you that this spiritual evolution of the human species is much more significant now than the physical dimensions of evolution. This project will focus on that transformation instigated by the shower of Spirit and how humans might choose to respond. But before we can discuss that with you, we must remind you of how a human being is "put together," how its various levels of receptivity to various frequencies of energy do—or do not—fit together. And we will discuss what happens when there is a marked disjuncture among the various energy bodies, as there is for almost everyone alive on the planet right now.

Receiving and Sending Energy

Think of a human being as one of those sets of Russian nesting dolls, each small one embedded in a slightly larger one. Each doll or body represents another system of receptors for specific energetic frequencies. The outermost bodies pick up the highest or most subtle frequencies; the innermost bodies receive lower frequencies. This is the case, in different degrees, for all sentient beings. It is, after all, the ability to receive and send energy that makes a being sentient. What is more difficult to describe and understand is how these various patterns of energy communicate across levels, and how the information encoded in them reaches the central nervous system to be "read" and interpreted. To sum up the transformation at hand in a single sentence, one might say the following: New frequencies are pouring to Earth. They present a new challenge of legibility and interpretation to the central nervous systems of many sentient beings.

You can think of each of these "bodies," or Russian nesting dolls, as a layer of receptors tuned to a particular range of frequencies. Different kinds of beings specialize in one or more particular frequency, but all beings have some capacity for communication across frequency ranges. One way to describe beings such as ourselves is that we have the widest range of frequencies available to us, with the fewest obstacles; we are specialists in energetic communications.

Humans have immense potential to communicate across a much-wider range of frequencies than they have developed up to this point or are using now. This impoverishes human life, blocks humans from recognizing their rich interdependence with all life forms on and beyond the planet, and inhibits individual selves from deep insight and spiritual growth. This we wish to change as much as we can—without undermining flourishing social and cultural forms.

Centuries ago there were many fewer humans on the earth, but most were skillful at reading the energies of other beings, especially the plants and animals they depended upon for food. Some few of them also became skillful at communicating with beings not in body. These shaman-healers played very important roles in these early human societies. They were the specialists, if you will, in particular energy frequencies.

Now the situation is very different. Very few are left who specialize in communicating on those frequencies, and many more—the vast majority of people living within the parameters of modernity—specialize in highly complex uses of language and abstract signs such as numbers. Regrettably, in addition, only a few are skilled in the symbolic use of language, for it is the symbolic that is at risk in many parts of the developed world. This is deeply problematic.

Most humans require communication at a blunt, material level.

Challenging information must arrive in large, unmistakable packages, such as illness, accident, a new relationship, or a surprising new scientific discovery. In truth, however, there is a steady flow of information into a human being's immediate environment that could be received, read, and interpreted. Incoming information must be screened, or daily life would be intolerable or impossible. Too much is screened out now, given the circumstances developing in the cosmic environment of the earth. Specialization was essential for the great leaps in human skill in agricultural and economic productivity, science, language, the arts, technology, and the other endeavors associated with modernity. The relentless focus on understanding how the material world works has brought stunning gifts to humankind. Now it must stop.

Human beings' focus must expand to include new frequencies, new forms of communication and information, and new ranges of sensibility and learning. Only then will it be possible to build humane and sustainable societies in close relationship with Spirit and with the non-material forms of life and consciousness. Along with many others, this will be your work now for the rest of your life. There is no pressure or burden here. It has been a theme of your life already as you picked your way through the strange practices and premises of the academic world. You have taken many risks to open to other forms of energy, culminating in what you are doing right now.

So what are you doing right now? You are receiving a very subtle form of energy from a non-material source, which you have learned how to receive and "read." It comes through one of your "outer" layers of receptors, is passed through to your central nervous system (i.e., your brain), and there is "read" and, most importantly, "interpreted." What do those two terms mean here in this context? You receive energy, not in language and certainly not in fine English sentences, but as pulses and patterns. You have learned to pick up those patterns, and in a place in your well-read, critically thinking brain (but not under conscious control), it is transformed into language. Because you use language very well, it is transformed into very articulate and clear language. We appreciate that, and it is one reason we have chosen you for this work.

When I say "transform," we are thinking of an electrical transformer that changes one frequency level into another, just as your computer does. A highly skilled human brain has many such transformers wired into it, and it is always possible to develop new ones. It takes receptivity, practice, and a great deal of psychological and mental openness. Most humans could develop more sensitivity to other frequencies of energy and could tune their own transformers to higher levels of brain functioning. If only 10 percent of humans each opened just one small window on a new frequency, all of human life would change completely.

The solutions to the pressing contemporary problems are not about ethics or markets so much as they are about better information. Humans are close to committing collective suicide because they have such skimpy, inadequate information. They aren't listening. If humans could find some silence and listen inside their heart-center, they would hear all they need to know to make the correct next decisions. Even that, the simplest form of expanding sensitivity to energy, seems impossible to imagine for most humans in the world you know the best. Yet you've discovered that even young students can "hear" that inner heart-voice almost instantly, if invited to do so. This can certainly be brought out into the world.

All Organisms Communicate

You should now have a better idea of how intricate the actual receptors are and how they absorb and process energetic information. Better science would recognize there is nothing "woo-woo" about our form of communication; it has a fundamentally electrical energetic core that can interact with cellular activity of your brain. Living cells are living because of the activity of such electrical energy, and since electricity *is* communication or the exchange of information, why would there not be communicative contact between beings of all kinds and sophistication?

Please close this chapter, which has offered a first mapping of some of the major topics we will discuss in this project. Now we can develop each topic in more depth.

|| Understanding Modernity

In chapter 1 we laid out some of the basic concepts and mapped an outline of human development and its relationship to larger energetic processes in the cosmos. In chapter 2 we will discuss in more detail recent human history (the last several centuries) with special focus on the development of modern science, technology, the nation-state, and capitalism. You understand this well and hardly need our teaching to make it comprehensible to you. Readers must begin here to situate themselves at a particular historical moment. Our point will be how this particular set of cultural values and practices has impacted human functioning, especially in terms of energy and communication.

The Task for Contemporary Society

Many people have studied this phenomenon; most then see the solution as a return to the values and practices of a much earlier civilization. They seek to reestablish the worldview, for example, of indigenous peoples in remote regions of the world—North America, the Himalayas, or the mountains of South America. It is one reason for the intense interest in Tibetan Buddhism in the West, but one cannot cure the imbalances of the industrial/technological world by returning to the practices of pre-industrial societies only dimly understood. That may be conservative in its truest sense, but it is a conservatism that ultimately offers no solutions. It cannot map the way forward. What is not moving toward new connectivities, new responsiveness, and new sensitivities is already moving toward disintegration and death. We will try to provide a way for contemporary human society to rebalance itself and prepare itself to receive new waves of energy arriving from the cosmos. Human consciousness must make a qualitative shift, so humans can recognize more of their own capacities. They are already hardwired neurologically, in both brain and heart-centers, to receive much more complex and subtle energetic frequencies. They have the potential to communicate on a broader range of frequencies. Recognizing and practicing this would shift much of the imbalance that is bringing human life to the very edge of self-destruction.

On Science and Markets

How has it happened that humans have created a civilization that carried within it its own self-destruction? It is not an easy question to answer. The very logic of science and technological invention is to be "value neutral," to be unconcerned about the values associated with the means or outcomes. This is strongly put but essentially true. One could say that since the seventeenth century, the West has experimented with the idea that objectivity is not only possible but is so valuable that it should be practiced in all significant human endeavors. That knowledge requires objectivity or value neutrality is the cornerstone of science, an assumption and never a topic of enquiry in its own right. It is a worldview adopted out of sheer faith, in one of humankind's most optimistic moments. Paradoxically, it marginalizes the very human being asking the question and doing the research.

The same is true for the "belief"—for it is a belief as much as any religious doctrine—in the decision-making of markets. Markets are valued because they make decisions, especially allocation decisions, in an allegedly value-neutral way. Markets allocate on the basis of efficiency and return, not allowing any distributive decision that might prioritize according to some other value. Again, there is a marked narrowing of analytic perception of what might be considered relevant to the question or process at hand, all in the name of objectivity or value-neutrality. The basic assumptions underlying the practices of science and technology are the same assumptions underlying the practices of markets. You could flesh out this complex argument more fully or ask us for further clarification.

Here we can catch a glimpse of a profound paradox at the heart of modernity: the two major drivers of modern society—science and markets— both eclipse the individual person to some faceless, disconnected integer. In science, the person is replaced by data and the "objective" analyst. In markets, persons disappear only to return as labor power, consumer demand, and capital. Markets work through competition. Persons do not compete; they relate. Only a sliver of a human being competes in a marketplace. Even in an athletic competition, only a sliver of a human being competes. Competitive markets reduce persons to a tiny bit of behavior.

The third place this appears is contemporary political institutions. Citizens have been replaced by voters, and politics is now little more than an occasional national marketplace erected for the purpose of selling particular candidates (or more rarely, a policy) to an electorate. This does not undermine the nation-state, given the support for political institutions from economic forces, but it has hollowed it out as a living form of a healthy community.

The Role of the Student

Before you begin, learned sir, blessed Manjushri, I would like to ask a question. Would you please describe to me what my best role in this work could be? A couple of days ago, I found myself thinking of questions and problems I would like to discuss with you, all related to this large question of the state of the human world right now and how it came to be this way. As I started to write them down, it seemed it would require a long dialogue or tutorial with you. What am I to bring to this process and this work?

Your full participation is essential, not just as the receiver of our language and insight but as the well-informed, deeply thoughtful person you have shown yourself to be. Our relationship, especially our working relationship, will evolve day by day and week by week, just as your relationship with Kwan Yin has. Please be patient. Some of your questions and unease come from some underlying anxiety. That will dissolve as we proceed. We hope you will come to trust this process just as completely as you trust your daily work with Kwan Yin. We forget that this is so new to you, and you don't really know very much about how we communicate with humans when we have the opportunity. We will also make sure you learn more about that as well.

We chose you for this work because of your learning, what and how you teach, the breadth of your mind, and your fluency with language. It would be foolish of us not to call on those gifts in our work together. You seem to see yourself as the silent, passive partner/receiver. That would not be optimal.

19

We hope this engages you so deeply that it becomes your treasured moment of the day and that it enhances your understanding, energy, and creative work. We expect this will be powerful and challenging for you. If not, then we have not shaped it well for you, and the ultimate outcome will not be as good as it could be. So we are very grateful for your question.

Please choose our topic for the morning.

The Student's Urgent Questions

I would like to tell you of my heart's grief about the world. There is much that is promising, of course. Africa wrestles with more democratic elections and tries to stem the spread of AIDS. The Europeans, even though a bit reluctantly, gather in their East European neighbors into the security of the EU. Both India and China have achieved significant economic growth, albeit in dramatically different ways, and there is reason to hope that much privation and suffering will be eased in both nations in the next generation. Slow, steady headway on behalf of women and girls continues in many parts of the world, from education and health to development strategies that focus on women's abilities to support their children. And there is an astonishing growth in NGOs (non-governmental organizations) around the world, doing good work on behalf of the poor and suffering. All this, and much else, is good. Too slow, too uneven, and too poorly distributed, but good.

My grief is about my own country and its impact in the world. My grief is about this global capitalist system, which wreaks such destruction and suffering on so many, that a few may gain. My grief is about the earth, and that our ways of producing and consuming are harming it irretrievably. As I often say, we are destroying our own precious ecological niche, apparently knowingly. It is incomprehensible to me. I grieve over the eagles who have left their nest of many years, because new property owners imposed a huge dock and new house right below it. I grieve because so many children have asthma because they are allergic to the air they breathe. I grieve because the glaciers are melting. Sometimes it seems my grief is as infinite and fluid as a melting glacier. And over and over I wonder: How did it happen, that I suddenly find myself a citizen of an empire, often a rogue state, which believes it can attack and invade any nation it wishes? That it can heedlessly trigger mass destruction, overwhelming loss of life and property, and even civil war, and call it "bringing freedom to the oppressed"?

I am sure all these sources of grief are interlocked, and if I had enough time, I could probably lay out at least one story showing how they are all interconnected. Globalization, global warming, environmental destruction, massive overpopulation, imperial politics, and widespread civil violence are all part of a dense web of oppression and suffering. My question for you is whether any of this can be understood beyond the simple answer of human depravity and greed. Does this have anything at all to do with Spirit? We have surely seen that teaching simple ethics hardly makes a dent in people's willingness to take advantage of other people. They build systems that systematically exploit others while claiming it is in the service of some god or religious value. Is there anything about human beings that can shift, such that we can learn to stop this insane behavior? Or are we a failed experiment in consciousness, a species that will self-destruct as a consequence of our having destroyed so many other species?

These are precisely the questions we intend to address here. Some quick answers: yes, human beings must integrate a rich understanding of Spirit. Only by shifting your standpoint from which you look at human and earthly life will you be able to see clearly the deep processes here. Is it a fundamental aspect of human nature to behave so badly? The short answer is no. In fact, there is very little that is "fundamental human nature." Humans are as shape-shifting as one would expect of the most successful species ever. The care of self is not in and of itself a destructive instinct but rather essential to every form of life.

The understanding of self and self-interest is extraordinarily truncated, however, and there are important teachings available to adjust that. Are you a failed experiment in consciousness? Not yet. Could it become the case? Absolutely. Are humans responsible for their own conversion and transformation? Not entirely, though surely one could hope for more sense of responsibility for yourselves and your earthly home. Will the Teachers help? Yes. This cooperative project, along with many others, is part of that. We are on the edge of a great turning point, and all the Teachers here are pouring energy and insight and support into every opening they can find on Earth. And elsewhere, though that is a very different story, and we don't want to get distracted here.

Have you ever seen a cityscape at dusk and watched the lights switch on, one by one, neighborhood after neighborhood, street by street, until at the point of full darkness, there are lights on everywhere? That is exactly what is happening now. The darkness has gathered, and from where we look, we see light after light switching on. At first just a few here and there. Gradually more and more. The darkness settles, and more people recognize it is time to turn on the lights. That is where we are right now. Sometimes the darkness fails to alert people that it is time to turn on the lights. Only when they see their neighbors have turned on their lights do they start their own process. We are not there yet, but will be, soon, soon.

So perhaps this story begins with your heart's grief and the grief of many others alive now. The grieving flows into a great river as you ask for help, understanding, support, and solutions. You ask yourselves and each other, and you ask Spirit. The unusual contemporary interest in certain kinds of orthodox and fundamentalist religions is a sign of this, for example. If you stay connected to your grief and to your heart, you will recognize these fundamentalists—Jewish, Christian, Muslim, Hindu, and more—as fellow grievers, if not quite fellow travelers.

Adjusting the Frequencies

First, let me answer your question about how our last session worked: yes, it worked beautifully. It was by far the most engaging session, and it left me feeling connected and part of the larger process. Much more of me was present, alert, and intrigued. All that was very good. Thank you so much.

Good. I also adjusted the frequency of energy a little, so it better resonates with yours. That is, after all, what relatedness is: resonant energy patterns. It usually requires subtle adjustments from both sides, until the best "fit" is found. You and Kwan Yin know how to find it nearly instantly. You and your friend become more skillful at finding the right place in the range, where you both are comfortable. You don't enjoy being with people who have only a limited range of available frequencies, first because you have to do all the adjusting, what you call "all the relational work," and second, because the available shared frequency often is too "thin" for you. Then there isn't much resonance for you, and you feel dissatisfied.

Advice for the Peacemakers

You have asked about the issues facing a non-governmental organization (NGO) engaged in grassroots peace-building work in a variety of conflicts around the world. This might illuminate how we see several critical problems.

The challenges the organization faces illustrate in microcosm what other such organizations wrestle with. Let me explain. The deep premise of many social justice organizations around the world is that political, economic, and social change must be created at the local level, individual by individual and small group by small group. That is not incorrect. Ultimately, change must be rooted in each person's consciousness and behavior. That is why the Dalai Lama teaches kindness wherever he goes. Because we are all interrelated, kindness is *the* ultimate, universal social value and practice, and it can drain some of the intensity out of suffering and conflict. Many social justice NGO's work on the individual level to increase the possibility of and the psychic space for kindness to opponents and enemies. This is very important work; in fact, it is absolutely essential. It provides a simple vision for people to contemplate and embrace, and it softens hard edges within and between people. It would be ideal if many more people in the world could commit to the practices of increasing kindness to themselves and others.

The advantage of this approach is also its main risk. In its simplicity and transparency; it bears no marks of any particular culture or tradition. It is in a way secular, though open to Spirit. It is markedly nonsectarian. It is infinitely plastic, available for local translation "on the ground," in a hundred different settings. It is wise in its recognition that kindness must first be generated toward oneself. And then it is doggedly local. It recognizes that kindness literally begins "at home" and spreads outward to local communities and beyond. It remains grounded and concrete within circles of human networks—families, friendship groups, larger kinship structures, local communities, and outward from that.

From Reform to Changing Consciousness

The very particularity of the emphasis on kindness, however, also creates a problem. The scope remains narrow, and it ignores power. It is time now to expand the peace-builders' horizons and recognize how their beautiful work fits into the larger global transitions of energy and consciousness underway. It must become central to the students' work. As they recognize their horizontal connections with like-minded reformers around the globe, they will also come to see how their work is entrained with Spirit.

Global social justice organizations switch on lights, one at a time. And more importantly, they teach others how to help people switch on their lights. The village-scapes and landscapes brighten, one by one. Progress is slow, and much of Earth's surface still looks very dark to us. Most NGOs think horizontally. It is time now for them to also think vertically. What would that mean? First, thinking vertically extends the consciousness work across more of society, to include elites and decision-makers on one hand, and the poor and marginal on the other.

The second way would be to think generationally, introducing this kind of consciousness work into school curricula, beginning with very young children. Look at your young Bhutanese friend. In many ways, he is a remarkable child in his natural understanding of kindness and relatedness. He is not so unusual for his generation. There are millions of youngsters in the world right now who have chosen to return quickly after difficult lives earlier in the last century. They experienced firsthand the terrific crises around the globe in the middle of the twentieth century, and they have returned to put into practice all they learned from that time of terrible suffering. These children must have sustained teaching and practice in relating to Spirit. They must broaden their identification with others, practice the exchange of self and others, and receive energy and guidance from sources of wisdom. The teaching may be nonsectarian, as the Dalai Lama teaches, or translated into local religious and cultural practices, so it can reach more widely.

This is tricky work. How can relatively "sick" adults create healthier education for the young? The work must be done. It is best accomplished by recognizing that the young, perhaps especially this generation, are uniquely prepared by their own karmic histories to jumpstart this new era of global life.

So ask yourself this question: What shall the children learn in order to work skillfully with the new energies, with the "shower of Spirit" arriving on earth? What is our human destiny, and how can we be sure we are moving in the right direction? Who really are the teachers and students in the human community right now?

An Invitation to a Quantum Leap

Let us return to our larger analysis. Humankind is being invited to make a quantum leap in consciousness, which will then dramatically alter human behavior. Quantum leaps, even for electrons, are very arduous energetically, though electrons do it billions of times a minute. Each electron must gather up the available energy, sometimes adding an extra charge. Then it propels itself into a different orbit. Being in a different orbit means it will circulate at a different frequency in a different "energetic neighborhood" and exhibit a different electric charge. That, in turn, makes it available for a new set of atomic relationships, if I may use such a word. It is the perfect analogy for what humans face.

Humans are gathering up energy, sometimes even self-destructive, but energy all the same. If they aren't adequately conscious or mature, they may be unable to handle it skillfully. The danger is that neurotic and psychotic processes or intense fear and anxiety may be triggered. When fearfulness receives such a deep energetic charge, it can fuel paranoia, aggression, conflict, and violence. That in turn intensifies the energetic charge for everyone in the vicinity. It is a terrifying cycle for those caught up in it.

At a purely energetic level, it is generating enormous amounts of energy newly available to human beings, both as individuals and in groups. The transformative opportunity here is to be able to harness and direct that additional energy so humans can experience a breakthrough, a move to a new orbit at a higher frequency. Then their consciousness can open, and with it, their understanding of their everyday lives and purposes.

If you cannot see this much-larger picture, you will misinterpret what is happening on earth. You will only see the suffering and the violence, and you will read out the trajectory and believe it is the end of human life as you know it. That is the error of linear thinking. If people like you interpret the phenomena that way, who will teach the young? Who will see this as a moment of stunning opportunity and transition? Who will bring encouragement and desire to the processes of human growth? Who will teach people to relax, to laugh, and to let go?

All you who work for social justice, all you goodhearted people of the world must find your joy and trust again. You work hard without really trusting that you are moving with human history; you experience yourselves as shoring up small pieces of social organization in the face of hurricanes of disaster. Your world and what really animates it must become much more spacious. You must learn to think cosmically, for only that will give you adequate access to the energy of Spirit.

Practicing Discernment

Good morning, blessed Manjushri. It is very difficult to hold two opposite points of view in focus simultaneously: the enormous crises on earth right now and your cheerful understanding of this as an unparalleled opportunity for increased consciousness and energetic skillfulness on the part of humans. It reminds me of the repeated message yesterday as I kayaked on the lake: "This too is a perfect picture of the truth of the world." Your advice about how to deal creatively with two very different points of view, holding them both in their related tension and allowing each to inform the other, reminds me of Jung's favorite teaching: hold the opposites in relationship and wait until the third thing emerges. Anyway, I am deeply grateful for your presence and your teaching.

I want to teach you about the sword of discernment this morning. All awake humans wrestle with the problem of how to discern the level of reality on which they are working and which level is the most powerful with which to address any particular problem. This is a multistage curriculum.

The first step is to understand how various levels of visible phenomena are and are not related. This requires backing up to gain a larger view. Then we will teach you how to see the interrelationships. Every complex problem can be addressed on multiple layers, but the sword of discernment helps the student choose the most potent and appropriate level. This requires very subtle perception and insight. It is time for you to begin to acquire and practice these analytical skills. This may seem quite remote from your heart's grief, but it is not. Your grief arises from your perceptions at a certain level. Within that level, your grief is deeply appropriate and meaningful. As you view other levels, the meaning of the grief and its appropriateness will shift quite significantly. We want you to be able to utilize this kind of fluidity.

Every being is hardwired, if I may use such a word, to view its world in a very particular way. This worldview is shaped by the need to eat and to reproduce, to procure safety and shelter, and to manage its relationships with the world. Over the eons of evolution, unnecessary information and the ability to process it have been discarded. Humans now, for example, have virtually lost their ability to smell, see, and hear signs of plants and animals, which could signal food or danger. Cognitive energy has shifted to other realms, and new aptitudes emerge, generation by generation. In short, perceptual and interpretive facilities, or brain and neurological functions more generally, are selected to meet the specific needs of each organism, while other faculties are left to be ignored, undeveloped, or discarded.

Three Essential Environments

You and many other gifted humans are at just such a moment: new capacities of perception and interpretation are arising in each of you to meet humans' needs to adjust to their rapidly changing environment. In fact, you are being stretched to add in one step three levels to your packages of "essential environments." This is one reason this is such a difficult moment for human beings.

The first environmental change reflects the emergence of a global dimension in new arenas of human activity. It is more potent than mere economic globalization with its global markets and trade. In innumerable ways humans are constantly receiving and sending information to and from all corners of the globe. Travel, media, information technology, markets, environmental pressures, global health, human migration, and global politics all play a role. Each intensifies the richness of contacts between formerly distant parts of the earth. Most people find this overwhelming, for they are not equipped neurologically, cognitively, psychologically, or energetically to process so much information or to be in relationship with so many new voices, values, and realities. This alone has fueled the increase in inter-communal violence.

One could say without exaggerating too much that globalization underlies a substantial increase in mental illness, accompanied by chronic diseases, family violence, breakdown of kinship structures, and many self-destructive behaviors. At the same time, the economic pressures of globalization are undermining the traditional institutions, which tended to social and economic distress in the community. Religious organizations, local and national governments, kinship groups, traditional health care, and cultural practices all struggle to adapt.

The second simultaneous expansion underway is environmental. You must recognize that environmental degradation in one region affects the neighboring regions, and that global warming is now literally a life-and-death global issue. Humans can barely grasp this cognitively, much less affectively or behaviorally, so they are stuck in a mud-slinging exercise over who is most guilty. Meanwhile, the glaciers melt. The situation requires a much more sophisticated understanding of the earth, from the hard geological sciences to cultural and religious practices on behalf of a life-giving planet. Individuals grasp this, but large social organizations and states have not yet been able to implement appropriate policies.

The third new context, after globalization and environmental crises, is that a revolutionary historical or developmental moment has arrived; humans are invited to open to new relationships with Spirit.

Realign with Spirit

It would seem that having a third major challenge at the same time shows very bad timing on the part of Spirit, for surely humans have more than enough problems to solve. So much learning is necessary now to understand how globalization and environmental changes really function and how these processes will affect human life, before appropriate solutions can be identified. Why yet another, and one that will pull attention into such a different realm? Surely humans should not be distracted at this particular crisis point in human history; must they also pay attention to the non-visible environment of cosmic energy and the intentions of Spirit?

Paradoxically perhaps, it is the reverse that is true. The "tools" (we don't like that word, because it seems so mechanical and lifeless) humans need to respond to new global and environmental realities can only be acquired by responding to and learning from the third challenge: the call to realign with Spirit. Humans must make the quantum move from one energetic frequency to the next, before they will be able to perceive correctly their situation on earth, particularly its fragility but also its purpose and meaning. That combination, plus the new energy and consciousness that will emerge, will make it possible to create a much more harmonious human society in right relationship with the natural world that supports it.

Let's say that in another way. We agree that the problems facing human beings right now are excruciatingly difficult and of a scale and complexity never before confronted. No one with the modern mind-set of contemporary science, technology, and public policy will be able to even grasp the interlocking cycles of oppression and exploitation of all species, now infecting human society as well. It will ultimately require a post-scientific, post-materialist analysis to understand the situation. It is not yet possible, though it is urgently needed. It is not captured by analyses of peak oil, global warming, and the rise of ethno-nationalism, for example. As Einstein said more than a half a century ago, one cannot solve a problem with the same mind-set that created the problem. That is precisely our point.

What is required is a radically different approach, and we mean radically different. The centrality of the individual self, which in this context refers specifically to the ego, to the little-self assembled in the early decades of a human life, must shift. This self and the cultural belief in it is an artifact of modernity, which is defined, in part, by scientific enquiry, the freedom of markets, and the construction of citizenship within the nation-state.

Little-self presents a huge challenge. We don't like to use the word "ego" because of its Freudian connotations. We are speaking of something less technical, "the invented individual," which became the obsessive goal of individualism. Simple individuality poses no such problem. The little-self has organized a human world that suits its claims to priority and authority. It has claimed decision-making authority in those realms of modernity, not so much because of its competence (that would be quite a different argument) but because of its critical role or value. That is what is at stake here: How valuable, really, is this little-self? Is it the only route to objective, value-neutral knowledge? Is it the best equipment for perceiving and recognizing what is true? Is it the essential tool for controlling unpredictability, for mastering threats to the self, and for assuaging its undeniable anxiety about its own longevity?

One must say no to each of those questions. Nor is it an adequate vehicle with which to address the third crisis, the demand for the quantum leap in human consciousness and human relatedness to Spirit. This is why this is such a radical task. Little-self has crucial tasks, but at this moment what is needed is a critical evaluation of its fitness for these profound challenges. You will discover, in a word, it is the claims of this constructed little-self and its hyper-individualism, which has been the single most important factor creating this set of interlocking problems.

One does not tame this psychological emperor by requiring a course in ethics or setting against it yet another finger-wagging, well-intentioned piece of the psyche, for that has been tried for centuries. Now we must approach it very differently. We do not try to tame this little fellow. We simply remove it from the center by extending the horizon of consciousness. Humans, or many humans, must be able to recognize the reality of non-visible energetic reality. Another way to say it: humans must recognize themselves as co-participants in a plan that they have not themselves originated and of which they are not the authors. This is not to degrade humans from citizens to subjects or from free people to slaves. It absolutely does not mean humans must return to earlier forms of religious practice and religious institutions that embedded them in hierarchies of dependence and servitude.

In sum, then: the radical re-forming and re-placing of the little-self is the necessary first step before the enormous problems of human relationships with each other and with the earth can be resolved. Little-self is not bad; nor do we think in terms of good and bad. It is that little-self is not very smart about its place in the world, and, shall we say, is deeply confused by its certainty about its own brilliance and value to human life. It makes us, the Teachers, laugh. Arrogant unconsciousness is also dangerous to human flourishing. This project is to teach you about this, as well as to contribute to its transformation.

III | On the Limitations and Liberation of Little-Self

We have arrived at the heart of the argument. Little-self, by which we mean that conscious sense of "me" and "mine," the place from which "I" is said, has been constructed over thousands of years. Most human achievements are associated with the increasing scope and abilities of this self. Many aspects of human suffering, especially those created by humans themselves, are also consequences of the increasing muscularity of this self. This must be fully understood now. Eventually, it will be clear why traditional religious understandings are no longer adequate for the problems humans face, for they were articulated when that self was nowhere near as fully developed or powerful as it is now. We face a new level of psychological and cognitive development that we must address, as we consider the major challenges facing humans today.

Self-Regulating Systems

First, let us make some preliminary distinctions. We see each human being energetically, as a set of multiple, circulating energy systems. Each is intricately related to its neighbor energy systems, as well as to energy systems beyond its own immediate orbit. Each local energy system is self-regulating, and in that sense, has its own center and its own locus of intelligence; it receives and processes information and then decides on appropriate responses.

Some of these energy-systems are within the material body, most notably the brain and heart-centers, along with those less familiar. Each chakra, for example, is a relatively autonomous energy-center. The chakras process emotions such as fear, desire, and love. They alert the human being to important activity on other energetic levels. They regulate the responses and fine-tune the equilibrium of these interlocking, closely related systems. Some energetic centers are not engaged in the direct functioning of the material body, but specialize, as it were, in higher frequencies of energy and communication; some are equilibrators, keeping the complex relationships between the body and the environment stable and healthy. Some provide what you call intuitive knowledge of others and of events. Some offer psychic peripheral vision or occasionally long-distance vision, not with bodily eyes but with an energy receiver sensitive to another broadcast band. Several specialize in receiving communication from what you call Spirit. We would probably say they specialize in communicating with non-visible beings.

Visualize a team of directors, each with its own set of responsibilities and capabilities, in continuous communication with each other, in order to establish the most highly functioning and well-balanced system possible. Multiple systems, and systems within systems, must continually re-equilibrate in response to information from the component parts; the goal is a perfectly self-regulating system. Please be careful not to read "self" into self-regulating. There is no CEO in this arrangement, no single decision maker, for no single locus of consciousness could be so skillful as to instantaneously and continuously monitor, adjust, and direct these multiple systems, reactions, and processes. We must say here we see this as one of the most brilliant discoveries of humans' long evolution: that a single decision maker is nowhere near as effective as such a process. This was worked out in thousands of versions until the most supple and sensitive emerged. It also provides a model of a profoundly harmonious world, in which parameters are recognized and responded to appropriately via small decisions and continual adjustments. It provides freedom, autonomy, communication, cohesion, cooperation, specialization, relationship, and sustainability. Everything is in balance. Selfhood, identity, and boundary recognition function appropriately for each organism within its ecological setting.

The Arrival of Little-Self

Then ego enters. If the previous description sounds like the garden of Eden, then the arrival of little-self initiates the story of consciousness. Virtually every society has a root story about this transformation, this new actor whose arrival changes everything: snake, Eve, coyote, or even Pluto. This is not, however, a new center of consciousness. It is the old, essential brain-center, the self-conscious aspect of cognition, which becomes increasingly skillful at certain mental processes and gradually begins to claim more significant decision-making, executive functions. To go back to our original metaphor, little-self, the self-aware aspect of cognition, proclaims itself the CEO of the team.

It does that in two ways: it substitutes its own decision-making powers for the complex system of decision-making already in place, and it eventually denies the value and then the existence of the heretofore self-regulating, semiautonomous systems. Little-self claims that distributed energy for itself, and with that additional reservoir of energy little-self undertakes increasingly ambitious projects.

What kinds of projects? Some are obvious: exploration, invention, and enquiry, along with agriculture, technology, science, languages, mathematics, the arts, culture, political life, and commerce. Some are perhaps less obvious: introspection, the study of the mind through meditation, the study of behavior, the development of the will, competitiveness, and even compassion and generosity. We could say much more about this, but we are moving quickly now. The achievements of little-self are impressive, perhaps most so in the West, where ego was first enthroned, but little-self is now a global phenomenon, and no human community is outside its realm.

There is no denying the many benefits of this restless, inventive ego and its imperial self. We could also describe all the mischief it has authored—wars, diseases, torture, oppression, theft, famine, and now, environmental destruction. But I wish to focus on the original two claims: that ego was only able to accomplish this by claiming sole executive authority (and with that, the sole seat of consciousness) and eventually by denying the very existence of the other sub-systems that make up a complex organism. The cost of these two claims is so immense, it cannot be calculated. The executive-ego freed from the information and self-adjustments of the self-regulating complex system of the organism must be understood.

An Organizing Image: Spokes in the Wheel

Imagine we are following one spoke after another of a great wheel, each time moving toward the center. Using multiple approaches enriches our

analysis and helps you form your own interpretation. We recognize your
need for order and coherence. Please be patient. Later your clear thinking
and writing will be very valuable. It is with great difficulty that we adjust
down to the human way of saying one thing at a time. Our way is to offer a
whole picture, the entire spider web. Humans are limited to one linear strand
at a time. So of course you wish for order and coherence in the assembled
linear relationships. We will try to provide that later.

Two very important points were raised in your morning meditation on
this anniversary of the attack on the World Trade Center: First, nation-state
boundaries and ego boundaries gained significance nearly simultaneously.
That is why it would be very timely to assess the critical functions of national
boundaries at this historical moment. Second, we need a rich analysis of the
political and ideological uses of the great monotheisms. These two topics
are closely related, for it is the monotheistic worldview that made possible
the contemporary version of self so commonplace in the West, and which
has undergirded the development of the nation-state as it has come to be
constructed in the modern world. Though there is much more we might say
about their mutual influence on each other that would take us far afield from
our current discussion.

Like you, we have been struck by the repetition of certain energetic
forms at different levels of human life. The tightly wound contemporary
self is reproduced at the level of the state and at many intermediate levels
such as organizations, institutions, and even family structure. Societies with
a concept of a more porous self also have more porous, extended-family
structures; it is much easier to join such systems and to acquire the rights
and responsibilities of those born within its confines. We might imagine a
continuum of porousness, with complete openness and fluidity on one end
and absolutely rigid boundaries on the other. One way to characterize the
long, complex process of modernization in the West is as movement toward
the pole of rigidity in terms of religious practice, conceptualization of the
self and the individual, and the organization of the political community.
Eventually the nation-state emerges with its emphasis on being born into
the nation, which expresses itself as the state.

Just as a thought experiment, contrast that with the fluidity and
pluralities of an empire or of a pre-state world in which communities have
fluid intersections, markets, and transport, and exogenous bride-choice.

Religious practices are often place-based, with attention to local deities and local rituals, but that practice assumes other places have their own local deities and rituals. There is no claim to cosmic or planetary omnipotence. There is an analytic link here with the significance of private property. Highly articulated systems of private property freeze the actual landscape through rigid boundaries; this can also freeze the social and economic relationships embedded in that system of private property. The system of private property may in turn provide a major obstacle to mitigating environmental stresses. Environmental problems rarely recognize the artificial boundaries created by social and political institutions, and in that sense, environmental problems threaten national boundaries in ways very similar to the forms of terrorist (which simply means, non-state) aggression against civilians.

Environmental Problems and Terrorism: Two Examples

This bears more thought. In our last session we spoke of the imperial little-self and how its claim to central control has so crippled the exquisite human processes of maintaining equilibrium. It cuts the person off from critical information about the status of surrounding energy fields. What better way to describe your current environmental challenges? Human communities—household, town, farm, river basin, lake—receive inadequate information too late. Another way to say it is that it takes a catastrophe to penetrate the self-imposed barriers or to overcome the threshold of inattention. A freely functioning self-balancing system, such as a farmer aware of the condition of her landscape, would be able to sense disturbances or dangers much sooner and thus would be able to adjust in a timely manner. The attitudes of self-reliance, self-importance, and self-centeredness are lethal in this regard, for they inhibit receptivity to critical information about the environment—what is around one—and that in turn inhibits an appropriate response.

A similar analysis is helpful for understanding what people believe is the sudden emergence of terrorism and its threat to contemporary political relationships and civilian life and limb. In truth, it has not been sudden; terrorism emerges when marginalized or powerless people feel profoundly aggrieved. If they cannot participate in the central procedures of the state, or believe they are treated unjustly, they must find some other way to communicate with the center. How can the powerless do that? They look for a vulnerable spot and attack. Their goal is not to win a war or even to stage a battle. Their intention is to communicate. That's why much of the heavy-handed "war on terror" only makes things much worse; violent repression is far more likely to trigger more violence rather than less. Declaring war is an extreme refusal to communicate, denying recognition as a legitimate participant in some political process or within some shared political space. The inside/outside boundaries are too tight to allow sensitive adjustments in policy or to allow for the million small movements within re-equilibrating processes. Like most responses to environmental problems, the "war on terror" is on the wrong level, misses the originating cause, and usually worsens the situation.

It is no wonder countries functioning this way are also greatly disturbed by immigration, domestic racial and ethnic conflicts, and disagreements over citizenship. The environmental analogues of illegal immigration and massive migration are global warming and spoiling of air and water resources. All are pressure points that ignore nation-state boundaries.

At our next session we will deepen this discussion on the forms of the self, and how the modern individual emerged and then was released into markets. Eventually we will need to look at the epistemological implications of this long process, for that has shaped modern sensitivities and abilities to communicate with Spirit.

The Self and Markets

Only this modern self, the individual stripped of his or her relationships to kin, family, ancestors, local deities, history, and place can be fully competitive in a modern market. That is a strong statement, and we will elaborate on it in this section. The emergence of the executive-ego culminates in little-self's claim to omnipotence, and eventually to be the sole recognized inhabitant of the human being. Ego believes, remarkably, that it can either overwhelm or deny the existence of every other part of a human being. It does not take long, only several generations, before the cultural memory of relationships with local deities and local forms of Spirit, as well as the practices for living peaceably and sustainably with various energetic-centers within and around each person are all lost.

Two additional statements are needed here to qualify those huge claims.

First, these are long and very uneven transitions. In some societies, it took a century or two to bring most people into the market system; they had to be "released" from the land and forced into the urban labor market. In some very highly developed market economies, remnants of non-market life can still be found. Secondly, people can be forced into a labor market or enticed into a consumer market without developing what we have been calling the "executive-ego." It is easy to think of examples, but the primary one is that working at very low wages and living in great poverty does not necessarily encourage the emergence of that kind of self or self-understanding. Many humans under such duress retreat to their embeddedness in traditional kinship, cultural, and religious structures. They are choosing predictability and security. This has fueled ethnic nationalism these last decades.

This revolutionary shift in human self-knowledge challenges our grasp of human behavior and human affairs. How will local people respond to a new market system in their region? How will a national government respond to urgent environmental pressures? How will a family regulate its reproduction with the emergence of HIV/AIDS in the local community? How will a solar-operated Internet connection in a remote village shape the horizons of consciousness, and for whom? The simple answer is that different individuals will respond differently, depending on age, gender, experience, resources, intelligence, well-being, and—not to be forgotten—karma.

The Impacts of Marketization

But our interest here is not to predict how any particular individual will respond to the opportunities and transformations offered by marketization, though gaining a rough idea of the big picture is essential to understand how globalization affects people. We wish to recognize how uneven these processes are, not only in different areas of the world, but even within countries, communities, and families. In the long term (a century or two at the start of this process five hundred years ago, and currently only a generation or two), most people will find they must accommodate themselves to markets and the new global system. This is why the stakes of this particular transformation are so very high.

Change is accelerating rapidly at every level. The social and political disruption to the daily lives of so many people around the world undermines traditional values and ways of doing things. The individual is wrenched out of his or her social network or never becomes part of one in the first place. Youngsters who do not grow up in multi-focal kinship systems with multi-focal decision makers do not learn automatically about self-regulating systems. They learn instead about "making it on their own" in a world haunted by powers and events well beyond their understanding, much less control. As we said, the first response is often to retreat back into earlier forms of social and cultural life. This is rarely a successful strategy, as that is precisely what is being undermined by modernity and its markets. It may allow some young people to move into the new world better equipped to survive, and in that way enable them to support those in their family and community who couldn't make the transition. That rarely persists for more than one generation. The other possible outcome, depending on local circumstances, is an accumulation of ferocious resistance, resulting in self-destructive violence, inter-communal conflict, and frequently, a long spiral into social and political chaos.

What has happened to the self from all of this? It is battered, angry, confused, and deeply frustrated. The world has changed in ways that seem to violate any basic sense of fairness and justice. The issues, the energy, and the stakes are now in place for radical politics; if that is not possible because of the condition of political institutions and processes (or the presence of an imperial or authoritarian power) what is thoughtlessly labeled "terrorist" in the West often becomes the next strategic choice. In that cauldron of rage, profound sense of injustice, and impotence is born the modern ego-self, the individual stripped of much of his or her complexity, in the name of physical and economic survival. It is a different kind of competitive marketplace than the globalizers imagine and valorize, but it forces reluctant participants in the market to become the one-dimensional, materialist competitors fighting over scarce resources in a very uncertain environment.

A World of Unintended Consequences

We are now in a world awash with unintended consequences. That is as good as any way to name a moment of intense and many-layered crisis and transformation. In the human world, real transformation usually originates in severe crisis, in part because only crisis can mobilize human energy to move to the next level, and in part because crisis *is* transformation, as viewed by reluctant participants. One can also say the reverse, that transformation *is* crisis for some, and often, for most.

What does it mean, to live in a world "awash with unintended consequences"? First, it names the major weaknesses and failures of the executive-ego. That little decision maker chooses goals and pursues strategies that seem reasonable enough within the frame of its own self-serving systems of "rationality." (Remember that "rational" simply refers to being goal-directed or in the service of a goal. It rarely has the quality usually associated with it, such as "clearly thought through." Quite the opposite.) Because both its "rationality" and its information are often extremely limited, unintended consequences are legion. The major claim of the executive-ego is that it alone knows what must be done and has the authority to make decisions. There is no need for complex multi-focal and continuously adjusting systems of decision making, if the executive-ego is in charge. With only sketchy information and the tendency to make decisions on its own, it is no wonder the executive-ego often makes poor decisions with myriad unintended consequences. No decision or policy can be any better than its worst information. And no one decision maker can replace or improve upon the decisions of an interlinked, multi-focal and self-adjusting decision-making system.

An example: in our realm of beings not in body, we communicate in webs of information. Each being is a node of an unimaginably extensive and complex network and as such is continually linked to constant flows of information and communication. The best analogue for you is probably the worldwide web, where each being is a computer plugged into the network. All the computers are always on, and nothing ever crashes. The flows of information are smooth and easy, and everything is simultaneous and legible. This is not a perfect analogy, but it does give you a glimpse into that reality.

An unintended consequence of some forms of sexual liberation is the spread of HIV/AIDS. An unintended consequence of the search for ways to ease the burdens of humans' physical labor is oil spills in fragile ecosystems. An unintended consequence of the widespread availability of antibiotics is the emergence of new diseases and organisms resistant to traditional drug therapy. An unintended consequence of instant, global news through the internet is profound emotional fatigue and the inability to respond. An unintended consequence of the development of democratic politics is the expulsion of wisdom and thoughtfulness from the arenas of decision making. An unintended consequence of easing the terrible oppression of women is that children receive less care from their family and community. The list is endless. Most of these could have been mitigated with more skillful decision making, resource allocation, and broader participation from the community. That they *are* issues reflects the prowess and success of the modern self. That the problems are very serious, some of them threatening to contemporary human life on the planet, is the unintended consequence.

The Fundamental Crisis

This is the deep structure of the crisis of consciousness on the planet; the knower and the known are no longer in adequate relationship. To put it another way, the dominant method of knowing, or epistemological practices, have become a major problem. Because few recognize that, the same analytic tools are applied ever more energetically. Of course, things unravel even more. What counts as reliable knowledge in the modern world? This is the core problem of the current crisis.

Summary and Review

Let's recall briefly what we have discussed in these last sections. Our initial proposal was to give you and all the students some idea of how current problems and crises on earth might be reframed, so you might gain a different kind of understanding of the forces at work and the direction and meaning of the larger trajectories of human life. Then we wished to teach you some better forms of analysis, including a more complex understanding of how the many pieces fit together. This is to enable you to become more skillful at discerning which level you are actually "at"—empirically, conceptually, and energetically. Much of our teaching so far has been to lay out the various levels and to indicate how they are all interconnected. This has been only a brief sketch, a first map, if you will. Eventually we will elaborate this first map, so it may be a richer teaching text. We want you to be more analytically expansive and skillful, so you will be better able to discern at which level any particular event is most "legible," and at which level you wish to respond. This is the crux of the "sword of discernment," one of our main goals with this project.

Brief Introduction to Ways of Knowing

To finish our first sketch of the map, we will speak ever so briefly of the immensely complicated and vexed question of epistemology. What counts as knowledge? Are the knower and the known related, and if so, how? How does the fundamental nature of mind and its thousands of permutations in individual human beings affect the conventional "rules" for gaining knowledge and interpreting what counts as knowledge? This will be a critically important thread running through the entire text.

One could almost say without much exaggeration that epistemological choices made in the early modern period provided both the parameters of the extraordinary developments in human knowledge since then and laid down the structures that would ultimately undermine the very existence of human life on the earth. That is a huge claim, which requires further discussion.

Humans, actually all sentient beings, have always recognized self and other, subject and object. Every human society acknowledged different ways of knowing, each with its own criteria for reliability and each with its own requirements for appropriate training. Reading tracks, going into trance to receive information from another level of being, meditation and rituals, training the body, studying texts, and training the mind were all ways to gain reliable and legitimate information. The community valued the full range of knowledge and the many methods to achieve it. Each community recognized that its well-being and often its survival depended upon such multiple avenues of knowing. Each had its specific uses, and each was valued in its proper place and form.

The Victory of Scientific Knowing

The early moderns made two remarkable "moves." They dramatically privileged one form of knowing and then rejected the others as invalid and even socially dangerous. The dominant form would come to be named as science and the scientific method, and its realm was to be limited to the visible, material world. This excluded the invisible realms, which literally could not be seen, and it rejected as invalid the means human beings had used to gain knowledge of invisible realms, processes, and energies. It would eventually lead to the suppression, often violent, of any person who continued to use any rejected form of knowing. Philosophical discussions of epistemological problems became increasingly narrow; only quantifiable and observable data would be considered valid, and only results that could be reproduced by any qualified researcher would be legitimate and true. Though it may not have been obvious at the time, this would erase meaning from public discussions grounded in supposedly real knowledge. It would also obscure the relationship between the knower and the known, because of its requirement of reproducibility. The knower in such a system must vanish, effacing himself and proclaiming his objectivity, a word that came to mean no knower and value-neutral.

This, of course, is utterly absurd. The knower and the known are intimately related and dependent upon each other as the two essential parts of a single process. We won't develop that argument further here. The implications are clear: this draconian claim about the separation of knower and known has led to many of the life-threatening crises on earth right now—especially the environmental crisis, the profound ill health of most communities and societies, and the escalation of domestic and inter-communal violence. It has become the most self-destructive claim of the imperial-ego or little-mind: that it is the vehicle, instrument, and repository of true knowledge. It claims to be the central subject and all else is reduced to the status of knowable objects. It is, if we may say so, the perfect triumvirate, each aspect supporting and reinforcing the others: the imperial-self, the philosophy of materialism that rejects all that cannot be seen and counted and that underlies the practice of science, and the obsession with rigid boundaries that rises out of the practice of naming everything "other" and which undergirds both the self and the state.

It is no wonder, then, that great reform movements of the modern era urge the dethroning of this imperial-self. We too will urge that, but only after we have discussed more fully this particular historical and cosmic moment. Many factors are coming together now, which must be clearly understood. Then, skillful action will be much more possible, for many more beings, human and non-human.

IV Why Can Things Change Now?

The more I think about human life, especially social and political life, I come up against what seem to me to be constants: violence, aggression, greed, oppression, and for most humans, ubiquitous and inescapable suffering. We are thoughtless, determined to protect our unawareness, and unwilling to respect the needs and rights of others, of all species. We have been this way since history was first remembered and recorded. Are the realists correct that this is in fact how things are and always will be? Is there any realistic possibility of reform, of improvement in time before we engulf ourselves in catastrophes of our own making?

The last several weeks you have been mapping a very complex picture of modernity and how the choice humans made to follow ego played out in many arenas: science, technology, markets, economic institutions, medicine, agriculture, theology, the arts, epistemology, psychology, and more. You say we cannot go back to pick up what was left behind, and that seems sensible in one way of thinking. But I must admit I am utterly perplexed and so aware of my own impotence both of imagination and action, at how we might change things. In fact, the dark feelings of my heart say there is no way to change things, that this is how we are, if not forever, then certainly for the last critical centuries.

Obviously you and your colleagues must know things we don't know and can't imagine. Why do you think things can change? And why now, of all historical moments?

Excellent! Excellent! This is very helpful. This is precisely the kind of heart-propelled question that we wait for from humans, especially from our students. It suggests the proper shape for communicating our knowledge and vision, so that it can be received by our students. You give us a channel, a route.

So why do we think things can change, and why now? That will be the focus of this chapter then. First, we don't think things can change. We know things are changing. We see it. We will tell you what we see, and we will teach you how to see it as well. Then you can teach others. This is our main purpose now. You must be able to "peer around the corner," so you can rouse people's courage and cheer. You share your sense of defeat and impotence with most of our students, and this becomes a problem in its own right. You are absolutely correct to ask that it be addressed now.

This is how we will proceed. We will first remind you of our description of how energy works and how humans are being prepared to receive new frequencies of energy. Then we will attempt to explain to you how being able to receive new forms of energy will shift people's consciousness, both in its scope and its perceptiveness. That will lead to new abilities to live harmoniously with each other and with the natural world. This will be new information for you, despite our brief introduction earlier in our work together. This means it is crucial that you ask questions. Please ponder each point as long as you wish and then return with your responses and questions. This may go slowly, and that is perfectly okay. We have unlimited time to lay this out for you and to help you understand it deeply, because we expect you in turn, when this material is thoroughly integrated into your own thinking, will be able to share it with others. This is our hope and intention.

Receiving the New Frequencies

Think of human beings as small radios, able to receive AM broadcasts. Then there is some technological development, and FM broadcasts are now available. Some will instantly figure out how to receive the new signals. Some will say there is no such thing as a new band of frequencies. Others will play "wait and see," to see if there is anything on this new band of frequency that interests them, before going to all the effort of developing a new receiver. Some will simply ignore the entire subject. And a few will recognize the opportunities the new band offers and go way beyond developing their capacity to receive signals. They will try to learn how to send the new signals themselves.

This last group interests us the most. The students we choose are all in this last group. Why do they want to learn also to be senders? Because they want to be in a community of people, of beings, really, who send and receive the new frequencies. They want to be in this kind of communicative community.

How does it happen that a particular person finds himself or herself in one of these groups? It is karma, and no, that does not beg the question. Another way to say it is that it depends largely upon the age of the soul. The old souls, those with the most experience of human life in its many forms and permutations, are those with both the most complex view of human life and the most openness to communication and relationship with non-human beings. They wonder, sometimes urgently, what more there might be beyond the immediately visible. Many humans come to that question, but few allow it to shape their lives, much less a succession of lifetimes. Our students are those who have agreed to that search for many lifetimes.

A tangential but perhaps useful thought: we have often noted that our students live most of their lives expecting that most fellow humans share their views about these things. It often takes many lives for them to let go of that assumption and to recognize the multiplicity of paths, premises, fundamental values, central goals, and sheer habituation that most humans live by. Only then do students begin to grasp they belong to a tiny minority. Some students never know anyone who shares their desire for life embedded in Spirit in ways not deadened or deflected by conventional religious dogma. Realizing this is helpful, for it mitigates bewilderment and self-criticism.

Each time a person, usually an old soul, agrees to become our student and to work with us, another light goes on. We see lights coming on at such a pace, that we are very cheered. And the more small lights, the more the pace of lighting quickens. For each student who consciously connects with us is receiving new energy at a new frequency, which in turn raises the frequency level of energies circulating around the earth. We will discuss that later. When students come together to share their work with us and to discuss the implications of the teachings, their lights come together and beam much more brightly into the earthly darkness. This we see too; there are more and more points of light. Yet, as your own sense of anguish and impotence reveals, very few students recognize how many there are or how many are strengthening their sensitivity to the new frequency and creating relationships with other students. Eventually, all will be linked into the great network encircling the planet, and like a huge astronomical dish assembled out of numerous smaller mirrors, the earthly ability to receive new frequencies will be stunningly expanded.

And who is not embedded in this emerging, complex interrelatedness? No surprise—political leaders, corporate executives, warriors and terrorists, narrow thinkers, and materialists, among others. Their world, dear student, is the world you pay attention to, the world you study and teach about. Every day you reinforce your sense that there is no hope of major change. Those who resist significant change are not evil or stupid. They simply haven't had the life experience to imagine the value of gaining access to the new energies. They are caught in the parameters and passions of young souls, whose major developmental task is to create a sense of self and develop an ego that will focus on what it perceives to be its own self-interest. Consider late adolescents and young adults. Their task is to leave their family, establish themselves economically and then to begin their own families. Love, work, and family, as in the traditional formulation. Only much later do questions about values, culture, philosophy, and ethics arise, the dimensions of meaning that stretch beyond the survival and well-being of oneself and one's kin. For every karmically adolescent political leader in the world, there are thousands of old souls quietly clearing out their own obstacles to a life rich in its relationship with Spirit. (This is most difficult for our American students to grasp, as the country itself is so relentlessly adolescent. One of the great benefits of having Mr. Bush as your forty-third president, in our view, was that he made it so visible. He was a stand-up teacher of how a privileged adolescent acts when given great power and authority.)

So in a sentence: the new frequency is available, and more and more students are choosing to receive it and wishing to learn how to communicate within it.

What does it mean, "the new frequency is available?"

May I say this teaching has so eased my heart and mind. I am deeply grateful.

It is a good reminder that you must speak out of your own central questions, for us to move most deeply and effectively in our work together. It does not personalize the teachings, but rather grounds and shapes them, so you can receive and integrate them. This is to teach you; this is your tutorial. It is not meant just to be received, repackaged, and forwarded to others. That would make you simply a passive conduit, which is not at all what we intend. Our students are sensitive and thoughtful; they require this teaching for their own development, which in turn will enable them to play a more significant role in the very changes we are describing.

The New Frequency is Available

So let us return to the phrase from yesterday, "the new frequency is available." What is this new frequency, and what do we mean when we say it is now available? Saying it is "now available" is a bit confusing, because it has always streamed out from its source. There have always been some, from time to time, able to receive it. They struggled to give form and shape to what they were intuiting, to condense it into images and language their neighbors could understand. Most visionaries and mystics have wrestled with that. It underlies some significant creative work in the arts. It even has fueled the lives of some blessed humans who taught new ways to live in relationship with Spirit. So, for us, the frequency has always been available, and for humans, there have been moments and points of access for the most gifted and devoted seekers. To put it in a very earthy metaphor, they were the very first kernels to pop. Now, the heat has been on so long, and the pot is so hot, that many kernels are popping; in fact, there is a great explosion of popping kernels, overflowing all the bowls.

The Impact of Modernity

What has turned up the heat? We see two main causes—modernity and cosmic energies. You would probably label one good and one bad. We don't make those judgments, because we see everything through the double lens of its original purposes and its ultimate consequences, a much more satisfying way to look at events, by the way, and we heartily recommend it to you. The slow and steady increase in consciousness among humans over the last centuries is a consequence of the same modernity that has also caused humans such problems.

Modernization and modernity have released individuals from their encasement in the collectivity. Each person must recognize he or she is in fact responsible for his or her own life, values, attitudes, and actions. This is necessary for expanding consciousness. (Some consider this to be a sufficient condition, but we do not, because skillful guidance and teaching are also essential.) Awareness of oneself as an individual, as the locus of mind and mindfulness, is *the* great step forward, as every spiritually authentic religious tradition teaches. The relentless and disruptive processes of modernization release human beings from their containment in collectivities into a precarious but ultimately essential journey into individuality. This becomes the psychic equivalent of becoming a wandering monk, who sought his freedom and followed his quest to discover his own deepest nature. The modern person, however, does not seek to discover his or her own deepest nature but is more likely to be motivated by the need to survive and flourish. As a result of that, the egos took charge. What you grieve now is not the emergence of individuality but that egos took charge. You and many other thoughtful human beings are overwhelmed by the unchecked rule of greed and aggression.

You see this—one of several possible descriptions of the contemporary world—as endemic, unchangeable, and a defining characteristic of "the human condition." We do not. We see it as a temporary phenomenon, the result of the merger of the many forces of modernity; individuals had not developed the skills to protect themselves from the temptations and promises of individualism. Perhaps the move from individuality to individualism is avoidable; we do not know. We do know, however, that everywhere the result of widespread, emancipated individuality has been individualism. And by that, we mean something very simple: there are few coherent limits to a person's activities according to the practices and philosophies of individualism. The individual has been extricated or liberated from his or her community.

All this you regret and criticize when you search your own mind. If you were also to search your own practice, you would realize it is precisely this social anarchy that has given you the freedom, privacy, and space to explore your own consciousness and ultimately to come into a conscious relationship with Spirit. We would suggest you think about this more thoroughly and self-reflectively. You are assuredly not alone in this. There are more of you scattered around the world than we could count, and nearly all of you have found some interstice where you could enquire and experiment and practice. There is no negative event in human affairs that does not have some unexpected, welcome consequence as well. It is an excellent reminder to cultivate equanimity and mental patience.

The very horror with which you view your world also contributes to the "waking up" of many of your contemporaries. Consciousness is very sensitive to strong emotions, finding them a source of insight and a marker of what requires deeper enquiry. This leads many to wider awareness. You share with many that recognizing where you are caught in powerful mental and emotional conflicts is also where you discover your own powerlessness and the absurdity of some of your most deeply held convictions. We are not going so far as to assert that the worse things get, the more people wake up. That is too simplistic. But there is a process here, which you might call dialectical, in which awareness of one's own suffering and the suffering of others often breaks open consciousness to new levels of inclusiveness. This is what we see. It is not your usual view, though it has often enough been your personal experience.

These are some of the reasons new energies are available now. Other factors are less driven by modernity and the pathways into individuality. And for that, we will turn to the largest view we can share with you, that the cosmic energies are available now to more and more humans in the grand project of cosmic self-awareness.

An Introduction to Cosmic Energies

Hello, Manjushri, sir. I confess, I feel some resistance to this next topic. I don't know why. Perhaps because it is literally so "otherworldly," or because it suggests a meeting of astrophysics and mythology. I know nothing about this, and I'm entirely dependent upon your explanation. That's not bad, just a little unsettling for me.

Yes, we understand. This material is often difficult for our human students; it is also the subject matter most vulnerable to the creative imagination of would-be mystics and visionaries. So there is ample reason for your caution. Just recognize it, and let's continue.

Consider that image you like so much of the swirling Milky Way. The "arms" circle round, rotating around the central axis. What is less visible in such a photograph, though it is obvious to an astrophysicist looking at the red shift data, is that the whole system is also expanding from that central axis. You also know your home galaxy is just a relatively small and insignificant "neighborhood" in the current map of the universe. We marvel at this, as do you. We also marvel at the human ingenuity, which could uncover this rich understanding of the universe of which you are such a miniscule part. This has always delighted you.

We would like to remind you of three points about the energetic processes that lie under the surface of your society's understanding of cosmic structures and processes. First, the universe as a whole is expanding through time and space, as humans conceptualize those.

(Let us leave aside the difficult idea for humans, that both time and space are interdependent aspects of a single reality, even though they cannot be studied separately. Perhaps the best we can say now is that energy can condense into a form that takes up and demarcates space. Humans call this form of energy "matter." Matter can also be transformed back into formless energy, usually energy invisible to the human eye. Add energy in the form of heat to water, and you can create steam. Cool steam by removing some energy, and it returns to water. It is basically how the earth works.)

The second point is that energy radiates. When waves of energy meet in certain ways, their phases can interact and either amplify or neutralize their frequency. Waves are sent out in all directions; from a single source we would expect the propagation of waves to be roughly spherical, with the intensity decreasing with the distance from the center. But given the nearly infinite number of radiating centers, there would be many opportunities for waves to meet; some would amplify and thus be able to travel further. This is easy to visualize, and reflects several basic concepts in Newtonian physics.

And third, we must add "spin" to the simple model of radiation from a center. The rotation around some apparent axis reminds us that energy rarely moves in "straight lines," and that the rotational effects account for many energetic shifts. For example, the spin impacts electromagnetic intensities in the field around the core. Parts of the system can gain a very high charge, which can enable it to jump trajectories or shift the path or frequency of its radiation. It is easy enough to say everything is impermanent and everything is in constant flux. It is quite another to recognize it is the fundamental structure of the universe. Any map of the universe is no more than a photograph of how it appeared energetically, for some limited range of frequencies, at a very specific moment. One can infer a previous "moment" by working carefully through those energy shifts and spins, but such inferences are at best only estimates. The energetic fabric of the universe, which is what the universe is, is far from static, and there is no permanent form. There is, however, a constant equilibrating process, such that various parts of this enormously complex system respond to and then instigate energetic shifts in other parts of the system. It is unimaginably complicated, and all the supercomputers that exist, linked together, could not provide even a simple model of the interconnections. It is literally beyond human conceptualization or visualization.

But here is the significant implication of this, for our purposes: the energy that encircles and animates Earth is shifting markedly, markedly enough that even some gifted human beings can sense it. We can characterize it as waves amplifying each other, or as a wider range of stronger frequencies, or as new frequencies carrying new kinds of information. All would be true. Because earth itself is a set of interlocking, complicated energy systems, what has been "normal functioning" is also going to change, sometimes infinitesimally and sometimes on a much larger scale. Many such earthly energy systems are already "stressed" as they try to accommodate to the first signs of the shifting energetic fields around the planet. Some individuals, some organisms, some species, and some species systems will collapse because they cannot adjust. Others will thrive and flourish. It provides an additional lens to understand recently discovered changes in ecosystems and climates, for example.

But our work is focused on human beings and how you are being affected by these cosmic energetic shifts. Why do we call it, among other things, "a shower of Spirit?" And what does any of this have to do with consciousness? We will try to answer those two difficult questions tomorrow.

The "Shower of Spirit" and its Implications

We have given you a brief introduction to cosmic energies, so you can intuit how energies flow to earth, and so you can grasp you are nothing but energies in form. There is no fundamental distinction between beings and energies; there is only energy, in many different forms, at many different frequencies, and with different densities. Matter is simply condensed energy. Humans are made of different kinds and forms of energy. It is no wonder, then, that humans respond powerfully to energetic shifts, though it does amaze us how unaware of this humans have become. Humans used to be acutely aware of the energetic shifts and rhythms around them, and they recognized they were embedded in shifting energies on many levels. Modernity has contributed to this serious and devastating diminishment of human sensitivities. Fortunately, there are still people sensitive to these energies.

There are strong new energies flowing from this expanding universe that are flooding human receptors. For those able to adjust to the intensity and broader range of frequencies it can aptly be named "a shower of Spirit." For those unable to improve their ability to receive and/or align with the new frequencies, it is perhaps more apt to name it as something like "impending environmental destruction" or the "end of the world as we have known it." The emotional quality of the naming will give you some insight into a person's deep energetic receptivity. When the new energy is blocked or illegible it is named as confusing, dangerous, or even world-threatening. And that is not entirely inaccurate, for it is those people who will find the changes unendurable or unacceptable, and in one way or another, they will find a way to leave.

Though these cosmic energy shifts will also affect other species as well, we will focus on the implications for human beings. Many who think and write about these matters frame it as a great choice for human beings, or that human beings "stand at a crossroads." It is not so. This is rather a long developmental pathway of increasingly sensitive and sophisticated consciousness. Although there are many significant phases in this development, we have focused here on the enormous changes associated with modernity and the development of ego, individuality, and then individualism. Most importantly, you and your contemporaries must understand the emergence of the modern self.

Just as it has seemed to you and so many contemporaries that the world invented by this modern self, this relentless, inhuman, dangerous world will completely self-destruct and bring human and perhaps even planetary life down with itself, it is giving birth to the next phase. (He laughs.) Yes, this does indeed sound like a confirmation of Hegel's understanding of the dialectic of historical change. Unfortunately, he was unable to make his most important insight clear to his contemporaries, for he was a century ahead of the moment when it could be broadly understood.

You see your world crashing in waves of biological, environmental, economic, political, and cultural self-destruction. We see that what is emerging is a much more conscious, less dense, and less intense world community. There will be better balance between doing and being. Systems will be able to harmonize with each other. The profound interdependence of all beings and all systems will become *the* major realization of human consciousness, and this in turn will shape human activities, economic and social organization, and cultural and intellectual life. Whereas modernity is marked by a stunning and thorough exploration of the possibilities of the individual self, the next phase of this eons-long development will be a similarly stunning and thorough exploration of the interdependence of all beings and all systems.

Paradoxically, this is not a regressive movement for the isolated self. Only the fully developed ego can enquire deeply into interdependence, if it is to become conscious. Nor are these modes of being in a zero-sum relationship. One metaphor could be the classic image of yin and yang, especially their dynamic interrelationship. This is a rhythmic cycle, a pulse between moments of strong individuality and moments of strong interdependence. Any move from one to the other is experienced as dangerous and confusing to those who must make the transition. On the other hand, it is the most exciting and hopeful of moments to those able to grasp what is actually happening and what its implications might be. To help people grasp that is your new work.

V Toward Consciousness of Interdependence

W e have essentially completed our preliminary mapping of the current situation, including a first discussion of modernity and how it has facilitated the full emergence of the individual with its many possibilities. We have also provided some of the essential elements of understanding energy, its enormous range of intensities and frequencies, and the complex adaptations all species make to accommodate to changes in energetic frequencies. We have suggested this is a critical moment of transition, in which humans have the opportunity and the necessity (depending upon one's position) to expand their receptivity to energies, allowing many to move from a life form characterized by the outward orientation of ego, of little-mind, to a life form permeated by a full realization of interdependence. New forms of thinking and social and political organization will surely follow.

This is not a reiteration of the simple opposition of self and other, as the major ethical systems have taught. Instead, that ancient binary will be resolved by the emerging consciousness of interdependence. Self and other are re-related in a dynamic process of interrelationship and interdependence. Interrelationship will emerge first, and then there will be increasing recognition of interdependence, resulting in new forms of consciousness. The conventional self or ego is not replaced by nor submerged in the other; neither vanishes into the collective. All three possibilities have been fully explored in recent human history.

Nor is this a project of ego and its ethical responsibility. The new consciousness will encourage new ways to frame self-knowledge and self-understanding. Ancient dichotomies and hierarchies of values will disappear, and a closer approximation to reality will emerge. It will require no ethical arguments and no conversion of morals; it will simply require a relaxation of the grip of the ego-self on everyday perception and interior self-knowledge. This will be the topic of this chapter, and eventually it will become an important theme of your work.

This topic too has several spokes or lines of analysis that lead into a shared central point. One spoke will map the movement from ego-self to self, from individualism to individuality and individuation. One spoke will trace more thoroughly what we mean by "interdependence." In another spoke we will discuss "species consciousness" and how that relates to interspecies relationships. We will conclude by pointing to the great ease, which characterizes this level of consciousness. And in chapter 6 we will describe several ways to facilitate this transformation and to make it visible. We will point out the early signs of this revolution in consciousness, which most of you seem unable to detect.

From Ego-Self to Self

First, we must begin with a bold assertion: the truth about the fundamental structure of life is the intimate relatedness among all beings. Another way to say that is there is only one system of life, only one plane within which equilibration must—and does—occur. Embedded within that single system are layers and layers of systems, each of which contains multiple layers of systems; one can go "down" into smaller and smaller units and not actually find any substantive, irreducible unit of life. We say there is only one unit of life, only one single system, but when we say that, we are using a profound concept of system that is not always comprehensible to human cognition and consciousness. The ancient Asian image was Indra's net, alluding to the profound and complex interconnectedness of all phenomena. You and your contemporaries might consider the stunning images of galaxies swirling out beyond the reach of assisted human vision, mirrored in images of sub-cellular matter. Such complexity cannot be fully conceptualized, much less described. Later we will give you some extra instruction in systems—how to think about them, how to understand them, and how to identify them.

The provocative implication of the fact that there is only one system, and that no life survives outside it, is that ego-self is not independent. It is not autonomous. It is not the author or the locus of freedom or free will.

It has limited access to the truth, relies on a dim shadow of what it calls rationality or reason, and is nearly deaf and blind when it comes to hearing and seeing its environment—its energetic environment, its multi-species environment, even its human environment. Ego-self has turned on its tiny LED light, intense and focused, in order to see what is in front of it, but the price has been to plunge all else into inaccessible darkness. Because it runs the flashlight, it believes it is free, authoritative, and powerful. It claims to be able to understand nature (the work of science) and the purposes of human life (the work of theology) on the basis of what it can see with the little flashlight. These claims would be simply laughable if they didn't also lead to so much suffering and ignorance and even catastrophe. Ego-self, the promoter of rationality and reason, turns out to be the most potent and successful mythmaker of human history (and by myth, in this instance, we mean fanciful narrative, not the deeper meaning of myth as eternally true accounts of the human condition). This ego-self, critical for human development, has strengthened the powers of concentration, logical thinking, organization, abstract thought, conceptualization, and rigorous analysis; it is also the major obstacle for humans to recognize the true structure and dynamic of living relatedness. The disciplined, rational, modern self blocks the recognition of the interrelatedness of all beings and the emergence of species consciousness.

May I ask a question? I certainly understand the critique of rationality here and its claims to omnipotence. I also recognize there are several "ways of knowing" available to me, only one of which is entirely encased in this center of knowing called ego-self. I know, when you say "system," you are not saying "being." However, how do you locate these centers of knowing, if I may call them that, and where are they located? In the individual human being? In the web of being, which you are referring to as a grand system of interrelatedness? In a species? Where is consciousness sited, and how can we know that? And how do we take account of that?

Excellent questions. Excellent. Too many for today's session. The quick answer is that every level of life, regardless of its simplicity or its complexity, is a center of knowing. Cells "know" many things, as they receive and send information, make decisions, evaluate their environment and their own interior functioning, and make the necessary adjustments. Organs and bodies are similarly skillful at precisely these same tasks. You are wondering about the next level "up." Does a species process information? Does an ecosystem? Does a nation? A planet? A galaxy? The answer is yes, and yes, and yes. That is, in fact, how one identifies a system: a system is able to receive and send information and make appropriate adjustments in its functioning in response to such information. The information is energetic, that is, shifts in patterns and frequencies. Much of this cannot be consciously detected by human beings. That is what makes a system a system; that is how component parts relate with each other.

Look. You have often heard the little story about the sneeze of the butterfly "causing" a typhoon on the other side of the earth. You have read about how human intention can change the wave patterns of a glass of water. There are countless observations now being captured by the highly sensitive instruments of modern science. These are, however, phenomena well known in traditional societies. It is the raw data, if you will, a flicker of light in the surrounding darkness, of how energy is the substance of all things. No corner of the single system is immune to energetic shifts in other corners of the system. Science has made you think of cause and effect as linear, but you know better. The arrows of cause and effect are multidirectional. Butterfly sneezes may contribute to a typhoon, but be assured, typhoons have a significant effect on butterfly sneezes! As soon as you start to see bi-directionality, or inter-causal linkages, you are seeing a system. Just because these relationships can seem asymmetrical (butterflies and typhoons) does not mean they are not a system. Ego-self is forced, by the logic of its own highly focused experience (and some of the premises necessary to buttress its own claims to primacy), to ignore or deny such bi-directionality and interrelatedness. And interrelatedness is not necessarily interdependence.

Self-Imposed Limits to Human Consciousness

All beings are embedded in multiple systems, which themselves are components of an ultimate single system. This has not required consciousness for this to be the case. Reality functions by itself, though that is an odd way to express it. Life begets life in endlessly complex ways, without the necessity of consciousness. Humans, the universe's main "bet" on the possibilities of consciousness among embodied beings, are not essential to the functioning of the universe. It would be a powerful teaching to invite people to imagine the world without human beings. They might be able to see more clearly the true position of people in the grand, interlocking systems of life. Bio-systems, you might call them. Human beings certainly are not a necessary part of the earth as a living system, and there would still be myriad forms of life if humans were to disappear.

But from our point of view, there would be a major loss: human consciousness. What do we mean by "consciousness," and why would it be a loss? To say it most simply, consciousness is knowing you do what you do. The more that is included in the knowing, the wider the consciousness. For example, you are sometimes aware you breathe. It might be only a simple focus on breathing. Or you could watch the breath move in and out of your lungs. Perhaps you can notice how it touches other organs as the lungs expand and contract. You can bring your awareness to a deeper knowledge of your physical being. Or you can watch your breath and note where it goes when it leaves your nostrils. Your awareness can ride an exhalation far out into the physical world. There is no endpoint where it must stop. Any human action can be known this way. This is the most reliable marker of human consciousness. There are no limits to the human capacity for consciousness.

On a theoretical level, this differentiates humans from other beings. What puzzles us most about human beings, especially your societies and cultural practices, is that in the realm of your most glorious capacities, where you really are only "a little lower than the angels," you erect so many artificial limits and taboos. You even allow bad science to be taught about how humans learn and how the human brain functions. You force yourself back into the limits of other mammals, who, though surely capable of real consciousness, are much less capable than you are.

Most humans, most of the time, resist expanding beyond those culturally defined limits to their own consciousness. We do not understand why you do this, but we see it everywhere. Perhaps this is something you could think about with us some morning. Whatever the reason(s), this is the major impediment to humans recognizing their interdependence with all beings. If they could let their consciousness expand naturally and without limit, watching the spreading "consequences" of any action move out from the center of the conscious self, they would be able to map the systems of interdependence. This simple practice is like putting dye into a circulatory system, and with a dye-sensitive instrument, watching the entire circulatory system become visible.

Someday you could develop practices to help people experience this. It would be a good way to increase sensitivity to environmental degradation, for example.

Manjushri: I am thinking quickly here, but I suspect that the main reason for this human self-limitation is fear and the human responses to fear, both rational and irrational. I am wondering if we might want to insert some discussion here of human fearfulness. I am thinking about the teachings I received two years ago about fear. I haven't read them in a long time, and I don't know if they would belong in this project or not. It might be fruitful to think about human fearfulness, not only as a limit to human consciousness, but also as a significant barrier to recognizing interdependence.

If There Were No Humans?

Yes, that would be helpful. But first, there is one last point to add, lest we lose track of this morning's question. What would be lost to the universe if there were no human beings? The answer is a certain kind of broad and inclusive consciousness, and this turns out to be very important indeed. This is difficult to explain in human language. It turns out that the single bio-system, to reach its fullest functioning and its most exquisite sensitivity to energies, requires self-consciousness. And that is the contribution of human beings. No other species can bring this awareness to the entire bio-system; other species can only process information from their own immediate environment and system. Only humans have the potential range to reach out to the boundaries of the entire life-system. And that leads to your next question: why would that be good or necessary?

Why Is There Something Rather than Nothing?

This is the heart of the issue. Everything we have discussed up to this point has been obvious; the evidence is right in front of you. I have simply been describing it to you in a slightly different language than you are used to. Now, we will shift gears from deep description to a glimpse of purpose or meaning—the *telos*. We stand here before the great mystery, the fundamentally unanswerable question, that gives rise to gratitude: Why is there something, rather than nothing? Why does the great cosmos exist? What is the overarching meaning in which all beings exist?

The simple answer, and perhaps the ultimately true answer, is that no one really knows. There is no being-mind that can so fully grasp the whole that it could also know the purpose and the meaning of all that is. Beings not in body, such as ourselves, seem not to worry about this question. For us, being is so full, so rich, so infinite, and so profoundly beautiful that it is blessed in its own being. It needn't fulfill some higher purpose. We rejoice over being itself, pure being, which is to say we are fully open to our identity and our substance as pure mind. We rarely experience intense curiosity and never doubt or confusion.

Humans wrestle with their curiosity, doubt, and confusion every day of their lives, if they have the strength and leisure to do so. We find that hunger for meaning and purpose is nearly a defining characteristic of a human being. Only a human would ask why the universe seems to "want" human consciousness to wrap itself around the entire cosmic framework. Only a human would wonder about the infinitely complex web of relationships that make up human interdependence with all other beings. No other being in body has this drive to know. Other embodied beings only need to know what serves their physical survival. Not so for humans. We have seen humans sacrifice their physical well-being to this quest to know and live out the meaning of their lives.

Humans are the primary bridge-species between beings completely focused on physical survival and reproduction, on one hand, and on the other, beings such as ourselves unconcerned about survival. This reflects two profoundly different relationships to form. Only humans (and a few other highly developed mammals, though less so) require bodily form to live, while they simultaneously participate in Great Mind or Spirit. We think it is this conjunction, which causes so much tension and complexity for humans, and which leads humans to ask, in every society and age and culture, what does this all mean? The question of meaning seems to arrive out of that tension, the complicated human double experience of form and not-form. And this drive to understand meaning, first on a personal level and then on a communal level, seems to drive the processes of exploring and expanding consciousness.

Does this help us understand why the cosmos seems to pursue, if not need, self-consciousness? Perhaps. For this might be how the cosmos can understand form and formlessness. How else might the cosmos look back at itself (it is not an "it," of course, because it encompasses everything) and see itself? It might not be the only way, but it is one way to dissolve the inherent tension between knower and known. Mind can know itself as the verb of knowing, if I can put it that way. The ancients articulated it as the problem of how to understand the relationship between the one and the many. That might be helpful here, for being in form is at the level of "the many." And the underlying level, visible with a different set of lenses, is the energy pouring into forms, constantly and everywhere.

So why is there something, rather than nothing? Why are there forms? It is the oldest question, and it has exercised many great human minds. The fundamental energy of the cosmos, sometimes named Great Mind, or Spirit, or the Holy, spilled out in its abundance and filled form after form after form. This imaginative understanding lies at the heart of every creation myth human beings have ever told each other. Energies sent out eventually return, from form after form after form. You named that death, about which humans have also told innumerable stories. The universal energy breathes out, into forms, and breathes in, emptying forms. Out and in, the great breath of the universe establishes the rhythms of life and death for all beings. Each being adds something to the universe's self-understanding, but humans add the most. Humans are conscious while still in form and can infinitely extend their consciousness. In that reach of consciousness, the universe knows itself beyond the original duality of form and formlessness. Highly developed consciousness reframes form and formlessness from a larger perspective and thus dissolves the tension between them. Or, to put this another way, one can say the divisions between knower and known, between knowing and the object of the knowing, and between subject and object dissolve.

Such full consciousness would mark full equilibrium in the ultimate system that embraces all that is, the cosmos of pure energy.

Energy is vibration, pulse, and rhythm. The ancients often spoke of the "music of the spheres" or "divine harmonics." They had intuited the fundamental nature of the universe. Intuition is an invitation to consciousness, to deeper understanding and expanding experience. The name for the next step now in human understanding is the recognition of the singularity of life in form and life outside of form. The major obstacle to understanding this is fear—habitual, unconscious, and unexamined fear. We will turn to that in our next session.

Interlude: On Buddhism in the West

May I then ask a question, not quite on the topic for today? I am reading a book of essays on Buddhist engagement with contemporary politics. I have been struck by a subtle, underlying theme there: that interdependence is the fundamental concept, which must be contemplated and integrated. Is that another way to approach much of what you are teaching me here? I would like to understand better the relationship between this material and the traditions of Buddhist teaching and practice. Is this relationship part of the apparently large movement to seed Eastern practices, especially those of Buddhism, into the West?

That is a helpful question. We will address it fully later on, when we decide how to present this material to others. For now, let me answer it this way. Yes, of course, this is part of the larger intention to integrate Western and Eastern understandings. The first huge movement was from West to East, in the forms of missionary work, colonialism, and modernization. East and West share deep roots in the teachings of compassion and loving-kindness. Those roots have developed into two trajectories of spiritual understanding, the great Western religions of the book, and the Eastern contemplative and devotional traditions. There are many ways that Jesus makes complete sense within the frameworks of Hinduism and Buddhism—most vividly in the teachings about love and forgiveness, expanded to include all sentient beings.

The return "pulse"—from East to West—is now underway, as you rightly observe. It returns to a culture that has largely lost its rootedness in the teachings of Jesus. Instead, contemporary Western culture is marked by its individualism, self-righteousness, and mistrust of the other. The elements of fear and control have occupied the vibrant center in many streams of Western religious tradition, largely in response to complex developments we have been calling contemporary modernity. The contrast between East and West is particularly clear in the relationship between self and other. The most effective teachers from the East speak about compassion and the need to open the heart, dissolve fear, and not allow fear to control human behavior. Ironically, if that is the correct word, many prominent Western teachers—Christian, Jewish, and Muslim—speak from profound fear. They lay out arguments about why their own tradition deserves primacy; they reserve loving-kindness for those they identify as "with them" or "like themselves." They generate more fearfulness and more closed hearts and minds. In doing so, they move far from the intentions and understandings of their most revered founders and teachers.

When we speak to you of the fundamental interdependence of all beings enclosed within a single system, we are addressing several dimensions of contemporary modernity and its long-term fissures. As a response to the Western traditions, it is a head-on attempt to present a deeper, more accurate account of how things really are in the world. As a response to the Eastern traditions, it is an attempt to break the practices and conceptualizations out of their traditional containers, much of which is rooted in local geographic and cultural realities. Many of the traditional contemplative practices reflect a spaciousness about time that contemporary people no longer feel. People now see this is very dangerous moment for the world. They cannot take the leisurely approach of cultivating generosity over many lifetimes to nourish the development of a single soul. Jesus urged strongly that new views must be taught and embraced in this very moment, that there is no time to waste. We agree with that sense of urgency: the classic Hindu/Buddhist view of cyclic time, of eons and millennia available to "get it right," is no longer appropriate in this moment.

We have chosen then to take the central organizing principle and structural reality of visible life forms as the theme of our teaching. That principle is "interdependence." It is the main topic of our project together, and it will be the main theme of your future teaching. The focus on interdependence can address multiple points where humans have gotten stuck and where their spiritual development has not kept pace with their political, economic, and technological skillfulness. Interdependence can serve as the conceptual underpinning of new thinking about how economies, nations, organizations, and natural habitats should be cared for. Interdependence can also frame new policies for global health care, the care of children and the aged, and compassionate support for all who suffer.

We will stop now and continue at our next session with a discussion of fear. You can certainly see how fear is the central obstacle to recognizing and practicing interdependence. Let me say again how helpful it is when you bring a question.

VI | Major Obstacles to Recognizing Interdependence

An Introduction to Fear

Fear is the most obvious obstacle to human freedom, the experience of limitless consciousness, and the deep understanding of universal interdependence. Every religious tradition and spiritual practice in some way is dedicated to diluting fear and its many consequences. We will sketch this out briefly for you, but it would be very helpful if you would also reread the teachings you received several years ago on fear. That will deepen your understanding of this complex issue and remind you that our current project has been underway for some time.

What is fear, really? Energy contracts and pulls itself in from the borders of its form. The energy, as it is compressed into a smaller volume, becomes more dense; it vibrates at a lower frequency. Sometimes it even shifts into visible matter. It is a kind of downshifting, if you will, from a higher, lighter frequency to a denser, lower frequency. This impacts every level of an organism's functioning.

For example, the lower frequencies make certain forms of energy exchange and communication impossible, both within and between beings. The compression also inhibits the organism's ability to recognize and respond to internal and external information. The constant processes of establishing equilibrium within the organism and between the organism and its environment are compromised when flooded by fear. Cellular, chemical, energetic, and mechanical adjustments are slower and less precise; this is duplicated on higher levels of equilibrium as well, such as mental, emotional, and psychological activity. Fear claims priority for the whole organism; all other processes must be subordinated to its requirements.

If you have just walked out into the street and a vehicle suddenly races out of control toward you, that claim of fear to be free to mobilize your attention and motion in order to get you out of harm's way is completely appropriate. But when is it not? When does fear's claim inhibit the well-being of the organism and undermine its best functioning? For humans, the answer is "much of the time." Most other beings do not experience dysfunctional levels of fearfulness. In fact, human fearfulness is largely an artifact of human cognitive abilities. You think, therefore, you fear. Human intellect and human fearfulness are deeply intertwined.

Thought, Imagination, and Fear

Human intellect and human fearfulness create a vexed situation and a vexed teaching for human beings. The fact that they are so intimately related makes it exceedingly difficult to dislodge and disarm fear. Fear is the major obstacle to the opening and softening necessary for consciousness to flow outward to all other beings. Finding ways to master fear and propitiate the apparent causes of fear, the fearful presences in the world, has stimulated the great rivers of human creativity and imagination. It has also led to the invention of hierarchy, greed, aggression, control, and terror. Fear, inflicted on self and others, is wound around the roots of human suffering.

Fear is nourished by human imagination. Fear claims the same cognitive ability to see and hear, to experience as palpable what is not literally present. Fear causes much human suffering. Some fearfulness, communicative fear, is a response to information from the environment about potential danger. Communicative fear does not cause unnecessary suffering; it does not inhibit an organism's high functioning; nor does it become the foundation for mental or physiological habits. In the following discussion, I will be talking about fear and fearfulness, *not* in the sense of receiving information about potential danger but exclusively about fear of the unknown or unseen, fear generated in the mind. We must study fear not as a response to an immediate and present danger but as a response to something imagined in the mind. Please keep this distinction in mind.

Animals do not imagine fearful presences. Nor does any other organism.

Though human brains and cognition share much with their near mammals, not so with imagination. Imagination turns out to be a critical power of human intelligence. Imagination requires abstract and categorical thinking, the ability to create and rehearse narrative, visual and linguistic capabilities, and very particular neurological wiring in the brain. All mammals, in fact, to some degree all living organisms, are able to generalize from a specific input to a larger category, and some are able to identify patterns and draw inferences from them. That is called learning. All organisms can learn to some degree. Boundaries are managed this way, for example. The human capacity to learn results in human beings' remarkable ability to adapt to new circumstances.

The most sophisticated human adaptive capacity is to draw inferences from what is *not* there in their immediate environment, but which *could* be there. That reflects a qualitative leap in mental functioning, which we usually name "imagination." It confers enormous survival advantages, but it comes with a price and a challenge: how to manage the false positives of imagined threats that do not exist. Humans seem oddly (to us) predisposed to take these false positives or imaginatively generated fears far too seriously.

The same mental capacity that can assemble bits of information and figure out how the solar system, the human cell, or the unconscious works also generates the belief in the vulnerability of the self, the dangerous other, and the dark terrors of death. To us it seems much of human learning is really an attempt to manage the abstracted fears of human vulnerability and death. I say "abstracted fears" because I want to distinguish them from real, in-the-moment fear generated by an attacking animal or a deadly injury or illness. On the other hand, these imagined dangers have also nourished the human desire to understand the world and to create protective social, political, and religious practices. That deep fear may well underlie much of modern scientific enquiry. How exactly does fear generate human curiosity, inquisitiveness, and inventiveness?

Fear and Ego

May I interrupt for a moment, please, with a question? Couldn't one say these human activities are also created to protect the self? Or to push it back one step further, that this fearfulness that you are describing as such a central part of the human condition is in fact fearfulness for the self, for the constructed self? That the knowing part and the fearing part of a human being are one and the same: ego or little-self. It may not be cognition, but curiosity and imagination, which are deployed to help bolster and protect the fearful ego.

Correct. Precisely. And the ego is nothing if not fearful. The ego is the locus of fear, the main source of fear, and the agent of fear. Ego's aspect as an active learner is its prime strategy for managing the local environment and protecting itself.

Now you see how the pieces of this analysis fit together. You could draw a simple diagram showing the complex relationships among ego, intellect, imagination, fearfulness, aggression, and unconsciousness, and from that, other forms of delusion and suffering. This would map the sources of human suffering, as well as the obstacles to opening human consciousness to the truth of interdependence.

We have arrived at a double dilemma: human fearfulness is both cause and consequence of little-self. How can we address human fearfulness in ways that allow for the continued functioning of little-self and without undermining human intellect? One approaches both through the same gate: the human heart.

The Cure for Fear

The human heart must soften and open. Then the mind or intellect can rejoin the heart-center, melding both into a partnership that can provide more reliable information about the world and a more insightful understanding of reality. The ancients spoke of the intimate relationship between wisdom and compassion, masculine and feminine, or yin and yang; all were ways to express this great human task—balancing, relating, and reintegrating the fundamental binary in a human being. We will use wisdom and compassion in our teachings for you, because they express the two highest human capacities; you and many others have devoted your many lives to its full realization.

Interlude: Being a Student of the Teachers

Good morning, Manjushri, sir. I seem to have uncovered a new level of commitment to our work, and unfortunately, a new level of impatience with those who can't make any relationship with it. I must ask you, please, for help both to stay focused and available to the Teachers and for patience and calm with the parts of my life that would silence this work. Perhaps this is initiating yet another reorganization of my life?

Yes, there is a reorganization underway; "reorganization" is your word. We would say focusing and deepening. To do that, there must be even more space, as you recognize. The shift this time will not be as painful and difficult as the last one was. Change will be easy and in fact full of joy, as you increasingly find your true work; you have searched for it all your adult life. Your work with the Teachers is the centerpiece now, especially this emerging new project with us. You are beginning to recognize its value to you, even with its mystery and difficulty and demands. That is good. We also note that it is beginning to seep into your everyday conversation. That is very good. That means you are integrating the teachings into your deepest personal understanding.

The Heart-Center

So let us turn now to this many-layered topic of the dance of wisdom and compassion and how it is the perfect medicine for unnecessary fearfulness, and thus, for nourishing consciousness. It is, as I said earlier, heart-healing work. But I must remind you, when we speak of "heart" we are not referring to emotions and feelings, as people in your culture do. We are speaking of the heart-center, both the central chakra, which radiates to all dimensions of human life, and the exquisitely human ability to open to everything in the universe. *(I envision a railroad roundhouse, the great switch system for the old rail networks, and he nods yes.)* Considering the heart to be only the site of human emotions ignores its stunning capacities for knowing, touching, exploring, and being. Emotions are usually reactive, a clue about someone's experience of something in its environment. That's useful, but it doesn't begin to capture the heart-center's capabilities.

Your culture also distinguishes between heart and mind, locating feeling in the heart and knowing in the mind. That causes more problems than it solves, for the heart is the organ of both feeling and knowing. When we say "Mind," we are referring to that which every organism participates in, in greater or lesser degree. Mind is the abode of consciousness or awareness, the source and continuity of being.

The heart-center is an organ of knowing—not of thinking but of knowing. Your culture has reduced the whole of knowing to thinking, and now you pay a terrible price for what has been excluded. We see the deleterious consequences in your society's education, arts, science, medicine, and even your economy. Thinking is just one route to knowledge; it accesses a very particular kind of knowledge, data driven, reproducible, and concrete or material. It rejects knowing based in the heart-center.

What is heart-centered knowing like, and how does it fit into this part of our teaching? Let me answer the second one first. Awakening and developing the capacities of the heart-center will be the primary way to calm fear, to expand consciousness, and to enable humans to meet the enormous challenges posed to them by the imbalances and distortions posed by hypermodernity. That says it in one sentence.

You might then say that awakening the heart-center is hardly a new teaching. It has been a core teaching for millennia, clothed in many outfits appropriate for many societies and cultures. Of course, we say. Why would the essential teaching for human beings change from one society to the next or from one century to the next? At some profound level, nothing has changed. And at another profound level, everything has changed.

Though the Teachers have spoken of these things for millennia, the purpose has always been to awaken humans to more and more of their potential. That continues to be the case: we see humans living vastly below their capacities, perhaps more so than ever before in human history. What is different now is that human life in your highly organized societies is threatening many life forms, including your own. Never has so much been at stake, and never has the boundary between your world and our world been so thin and permeable.

Though the risks are great, the opportunities are great as well. We teach what we teach because it reflects our own being, which is life from the heart-center. That is what characterizes the teachers of Spirit—beings entirely formed by and living from their heart-center. That is why we are the best teachers for people now about to make the transition to living from their heart-center. That is the path of the bodhisattva made new for your postmodern, suffering world.

Tomorrow we will discuss with you the obstacles in your society and culture to awakening and valuing the heart-center. Then we will begin a new chapter on the heart-center and how it can awaken.

The Absence of the Heart-Center from Public Life

The heart-center has disappeared from American public life. Our analysis will also be true for many other parts of the world as well. This is not new information for many students. It will reframe and rename it, giving new leverage for thinking and responding in creative and powerful ways.

First, you must see that the heart-center barely functions in American public and political life. What we see is the dominance of a very limited kind of cognition in service to self-protection, self-aggrandizement, and control of others. In other words, your world is awash in defensiveness, greed, and aggression, maintained by unchecked and irrational fear. That which we have been discussing on the individual level defines the public level as well; fear courses through political institutions, economic and corporate institutions, public entertainment and the media.

American institutions now, without exception, are shaped by what they perceive to be the necessity of winning in a dangerous and highly competitive marketplace. The first and last question is always how can I take advantage of this situation? How can I best mobilize my resources to be successful in this relentless competition? Decision makers in organizations and institutions will recognize those pressures, and most will add that they find them distasteful and misleading; leaders recognize how much long-term damage results. Sadly, most will also confess they feel powerless to ignore the rules of the game. In what is allegedly the nation founded on freedom, competent leaders feel powerless to act as they wish, because the system has so imprisoned them. Very few Americans believe they are able to act on the basis of their deepest values, and those few are likely to be either the very rich or the voluntarily poor protected within religious institutions. What has so empowered this mad competition and allowed it to penetrate so deeply into American life?

The simple answer is competitive markets, especially in arenas completely inappropriate for market decision making. How do competitive markets affect normal human functioning, especially the ability to live from the heart-center? From what we observe, it seems to make it nearly impossible, or only possible at a very high personal price; only the most evolved are able to maintain their access to their own deep center. It has become rare (indeed, heroic) in your culture to live from the heart. That is absurd. No society can survive very well that way, much less remain intact for several generations. You and many others are aware of the deep rot, the consequence of atrophied heart-centers, undermining many American institutions and practices.

Markets Constrict Human Life

The aggressive penetration of markets deeper and deeper into social and public life has caused more and more people, more and more often, to choose to function with the parts of themselves that seem to promise the best advantage in those markets. In a labor market, people will emphasize their ability to contribute to profits. In an entertainment market, people will emphasize their appeal to the largest audience by providing what they imagine to be in the greatest demand: violence, consumerism, sex, and other forms of uncomplicated pleasures. This is, ironically, a projection of their own unconscious selves, and because unrecognized, assumed to be what is desired in the mass market. The same is true in political life, where unconscious projections combine with mass marketing, drowning out discussions essential to democratic politics and policy-making. Similar forces are at work in economic life, where the bottom line shapes corporate behavior. Since the bottom line is redefined, day by day, it is no longer possible to pursue long-term corporate goals such as long-term profitability, stable supply lines, a skilled workforce, preservation of the resource base, and the local environment. Long-term priorities cannot compete when investor return (i.e., the price of shares) is the only measure of corporate success.

Summary

This chapter has discussed the most significant obstacles for people to recognize their interdependence with each other and the other species of the earth. Fear, not the species-appropriate fear of specific threats in the environment, but the fear generated by little-self, the ego, is the fundamental issue. Ego-manufactured fear is rooted in the imaginative capacities of human beings, the shadow side of the enormously creative and flexible human intellect.

Fear generates much social and political behavior in your society, which in turn inhibits the awareness of interdependence. We have focused particularly on competitive markets and their penetration into arenas never before subjected to marketization. This process too is driven by fear and its close collaborator, aggression. People cannot live from their heart-centers, having been taught either that there is no such thing or that its judgment is foolish or even self-destructive.

Yet living from the heart-center is the solution to your world's enormous problems. The new teachers emerging into view are equipped to address these complex social, political, and human issues. They can identify the dangerous failures of perception and evaluation. They are teachers of the heart, and their purpose is to call to the hearts of those around them. They will support the difficult tasks of learning to listen to the heart-center and allowing it to shape critical decisions.

One more time, let us remind you we are not speaking of stimulating more feeling or emotional responses, though that will happen naturally as part of this awakening and healing. When we say "heart-center," we refer to that seat of consciousness at the center of the human person that is informed both by deep values and a complex understanding of the real world. It is the nexus where knowledge and human feelings are brought together to nourish and direct a richer and more inclusive understanding of people in their community, the earth, and the universe. It is the seat of meaning, where meaning is recognized and embraced.

VII | The Heart-Center

Interlude: A Question on Method

*B*efore we begin our usual work, Manjushri, sir, may I ask a question? I'm wondering, what is my role here? How shall I engage with and on behalf of these teachings?

Those are very good questions. We recognize your concern about protecting the energy that moves through these ideas, and that is appropriate and important. There are several ways to handle this. For now, we would prefer that you simply receive the teachings, write them down, and then read and meditate on them, until you know them deeply. Of course, the text could be edited and revised. That would be a lot of work for you, and we aren't certain that is the best thing for you this year. We would rather you be free to write other things, to explore other dimensions of this great transformation, and to find ways to bring the initial messages out into the world. This is nearing a natural closure, probably within a week or two. We will have some advice for you about what to do next.

Responding to the New Energy

So let's recall briefly where we began. First, humans are evolutionarily responsive in two dimensions: genetically or physiologically, and energetically or spiritually. These are tricky words, but let's just use them for the moment. Second, new energy with higher and more intense frequencies is arriving on earth, stimulating adaptive responses by many species, most especially by humans. This reflects aspects of the nature of mind and human consciousness and what might be called the ultimate intention of Spirit. Questions then arise: what kinds of human responses to the new energy are possible, which are most appropriate, and how can some of you assist others to make these transitions smoothly and skillfully?

Because humans are such complex creatures, many responses are possible. We will describe them briefly so you can learn to recognize them. This will also help you appreciate how humans differ in their psychological, intellectual, and energetic development. You tend to see all humans as basically similar, which is not entirely accurate.

Every human, actually every organism, experiences the shifts in energy arriving from outside the earth's atmosphere. Most energy shifts are very subtle, and even highly evolved humans sometimes fail to recognize them. That is no surprise, for it is analogous to asking fish to notice subtle changes in their water world. These processes can be both subtle and substantial simultaneously, for "subtle" refers to the sensitivity of the receiver, not the significance of the phenomenon.

Some acutely sensitive people, usually highly evolved as well, recognize the shifts and nearly automatically adjust their life rhythms to the new frequencies. They might change their meditation practice, their diet, their level of physical activity, or the balance between solitude and non-solitude, for example. Some individuals will find other ways to adjust their receptivity, so as to be "in phase," if you will pardon a technical term, with the shifting energy patterns. When someone accomplishes that, she or he will find renewed physical and creative energy, more ease in daily activities, and a richer realization of living in the larger cosmos.

Not being in phase sets off a variety of discomforts or intensifies previous points of conflict or unease. Chronic illness, for example, can worsen. Daily currents of irritability or non-cooperativeness can be generated or intensified by this phenomenon. Organisms experience extra difficulty with some functions, such as immune responses, digestion, respiration, emotional processing, and communication, as well as higher-order processes such as cognition, analysis, intuition, and judgment. It's not that these can't be managed, for they often can. It simply requires more attentiveness and effort. Sometimes that is possible, and sometimes not. When it is not possible, the organism might weaken, fail to reproduce, or even die. It is then part of a larger evolutionary process, which selects those organisms most skillful at adjusting and responding to the energy shifts in the environment. I say both adjust and respond because though all organisms must adjust, eventually only the most complex can also respond. By respond I mean they are able to integrate the new energy into their own systems and use it as they choose. Eventually we will want to discuss that more fully, for that is the very crux of the matter under discussion in this entire project.

To return to our main point: this heightened stress on many beings has exacerbated the critical long-term problems humans face in providing themselves with adequate subsistence, the endemic struggles over scarce resources, overpopulation, disease, and now, rapidly deteriorating environmental health. Problems and conflicts, which might have simmered along relatively quietly for centuries, now erupt into floods of aggression and suffering. One consequence is that many who are deeply afflicted by disease, hunger, and war are also those least able to respond to the new conditions. Though this is very difficult for people to accept, it is not necessarily regrettable that many leave now in order to return better able to generate and exercise new capabilities.

A Question about Suffering and Karma

May I ask a question then? It seems that this process is nearly circular: the inability to adapt intensifies the challenges to the organism, which in turn undermines its ability to adapt. If so, how could one possibly shift or exit that vicious cycle? Only through death and rebirth? If that is the case, nothing we can do now, while in body, would make much difference.

Good question, but your answer is too limiting. Again, one must remember there are different degrees of adaptive skillfulness. We see you resist any explanation that seems to blame those who suffer most, or even which holds them somehow responsible for their own dead ends and vicious cycles. But that describes the human condition, as the great teachers have taught. Suffering is endemic, even though humans can perceive, judge, and act differently. Humans have capabilities they rarely exercise, and the main purpose of multiple lives is to develop and exercise those capabilities. On the way, humans continue to dissolve the obstacles to fuller functioning. What you see before you is actually a reflection of differences in age, age in spirit, or degree of development. There is no need to posit other worlds in which beings are either rewarded or suffer for their behavior on earth. Human beings create their world right here, in the lives they live. Multiple lives allow the curriculum to unfold and students to advance, one step at a time. What is different about the present moment is that the entire earth is receiving a new, stepped-up energy, and just as some chemical reactions can speed up with more heat, many human psychic, cognitive, spiritual, and emotional reactions are speeding up under the influence of the new energies arriving from outside the planetary system.

By the way, this is not some long-awaited messiah, not the deliverer, not an angelic messenger or any other mythical being expected on the eve of the next great transformation or heavenly denouement. The great historic visionaries glimpsed the possibility of profound transformation and spoke of it to their communities in terms of mythic heroes and saviors. There is certainly heroic and salvific work here, but it is each being learning and developing lifetime by lifetime. What is more heroic than the quest for fuller consciousness? What is more salvific than recognizing the interdependence of all beings and then acting accordingly? It is all there, in the ancient myths.

Some beings are profoundly frightened of this process. Their anxiety and insecurity fuel aggression and violence, visible around the world. That fearfulness is an accurate marker of disability and the inability to adjust to the new frequencies and their new demands. On the other hand, the main marker of the new frequencies is much greater opportunity for communication and relatedness.

Some beings are not so much frightened as blasé; they recognize something is shifting and are curious, but they don't recognize any implications for themselves. They consider it irrelevant, without any personal resonance or meaning. Many people of adequate education or relatively well-developed religious sensibilities belong in this group. They seem to understand, but in the end, it doesn't result in any personal change. They don't take much responsibility for themselves or their world; their worldview is often too narrow and rigid.

The responders recognize the changes and their implications for themselves and their communities. Their understanding of interdependence is the measure of where they are on this long path to full consciousness and what they are likely to accomplish in this and future lifetimes.

Interlude: Naming the Conversation

Good morning, Manjushri. I have another pressing question. I have been experimenting with describing this new work to several colleagues, and I think I am getting somewhere. I am not saying I am channeling it or that you are sending it to me, or anything so explicit. I describe sitting quietly, waiting for language to start to rise up, and then I just write down what comes. One friend nodded and said, "Yes, you are writing from your heart rather than from your head." Another named it "Inspiration! Many writers have reported that." In other words, I allow my listener to name it in her own words. I don't think I'm lying, but I am certainly not telling the whole truth. It makes me uneasy because I am not naming the real source of all of this.

Thank you for the question. You are speaking more truth than perhaps you realize. Your question assumes two ontologically separate beings, you and "me." But that is not really the case, not the way you frame it in your conventional Western concepts; subject/object is not an adequate framework for these questions. Your consciousness participates intimately in mine; viewed from another direction, mine participates in yours. The most accurate is that both of our consciousnesses participate in the great One Mind, where subject and object are never fully distinguishable. In our work together, you open to our consciousness, and there is something akin to what the Tibetans call "direct transmission." A fundamental concept or image is made available to you, and you process it and translate it into language. Your language brain works like a transformer, ratcheting the 220 current down to 110, so what you receive can be expressed in language. That, by the way, is one of the reasons the work is so tiring; your system has to absorb all the unused energy. Perhaps more than you realize, this is indeed your life work. It is not the work of your focused intellect, but of your spirit as it listens and speaks through your heart-center.

This ability to speak through the heart-center is available to most humans. The great pity is that so few do. All it requires, as you now know, is the ability to quiet the cognitive mind and little-self, so one can listen to the heart. It is simple to teach and simple to learn. The difficulty is getting people to practice regularly enough that they can override the cultural chatter and baggage of contemporary life. So much public discourse is predicated on falsehoods about the self, language, perception, and insight. The narrow epistemology so characteristic of modernity is really what most blocks human development and the expansion of human consciousness.

So to return to your question: we encourage you to develop multiple ways to help people open to these ideas and this material. Imagine that you are building bridges, often personally tailored for each listener, so she can develop a richer and more inclusive understanding of human reality. Most spiritual teachers have wrestled with these problems, and most turn to image, metaphor, narrative, and myth for help. Skillful teachers use every available tool to help them communicate the essential truth to their students. Different students require different forms, as you know from your own classroom. This is hardly the moment to embrace positivism with its simple-minded dualisms. Let that go, please. Tell each person as much as you possibly can, but don't make the message unacceptable because of your desire to say more than necessary. Don't be obsessed with authorship. There is much less authorship than meets the eye; we are removing obstacles to your ability to see clearly. New shapes emerge, making visible new processes and relationships, precisely what one would expect from clearer vision and more sensitive listening. Every human has access to the very same power. That is the main reason you are finding these ideas in many forms all around you. We are providing this teaching in many versions and languages, all around the earth. It is simply time.

Opening the Heart-Center

Now let us return to the main topic of this section: ways for humans to open their heart-center, strengthen it, and improve their ability to listen, to communicate, and to discern and live from their heart-centers. Since virtually all blockages are rooted in fear, we will now take up that very large problem. We have already distinguished between two kinds of fear—the fear that is useful to the organism, in that it communicates proximate danger, and the fear created by the imagination, something peculiar to humans and a few other highly developed primates and domesticated mammals. It is the latter fear we will be discussing here. Please keep that in mind.

Language and cultural practices are the two most powerful ways to teach people specific fears. As you move through your days, watch for examples of this. Fearfulness is encoded in advertising and in common images of the other. The word "terrorist," for example, is used so frequently that it has lost its descriptive power. Fear stars in mainstream forms of entertainment. Consider all the violent images and stories about violence just on the major networks, not to mention popular music, films, and other media. Every person is saturated with images intended to provoke fear. You all live in a state of hyper-arousal from this ubiquitous presentation of frightening people and events. First the fear is stimulated and then its "fix"—a product, a candidate, a sports star, a new drug—is offered. You can see this in your public cultural practices. The media have become the major instigators and maintainers of fear, with consumerism and the marketplace routinely presented as the solution.

Let us return to our main point: it is this pervasive fearfulness (and the double responses of consumerism and aggression) that most obstructs humans from living from their heart-centers. Fear prevents humans from recognizing their interdependence with other humans and with other species. Because of fear, people adopt behaviors and implement public policies meant to mitigate its alleged consequences. This strategy fails, and most of these remedies in fact intensify the original fear and its underlying anxiety. Life is not under the control of little-self or the ego. Ego is the part of the personality defined by its premise that it should control all risk. It is also that part of the personality that both generates and reiterates fear in order to justify its own importance. We discover again the cycle that generates so much human confusion and suffering. Ignorance about reality—both of the person and the world around her—leads to cycles of incorrect predictions that trigger inappropriate defenses and responses, leading to more misinformation as the end result. More and more human capabilities are shut down in order to sustain the position of the ego. Even if ego would like to change, to become more kind and generous and to live in a less violent world, it doesn't really know how. The whole earth could be papered in books claiming to be a roadmap, but unfortunately they usually argue it is simply a matter of choosing the good and acting on it.

Nothing could be further from the truth. As we have said before, this is *not* a question of ethics or moral behavior, of putting the other before self. It is a question of accurate, precise information about how things really are, about how a human being is constituted, and what optimal human functioning is like. There are so few highly functioning human beings in your media-saturated world, that most of you have never even heard or met such a person. Because you can't imagine what is humanly possible, you are persuaded to suppress potentially skillful responses in order to manage the fear. To us, this is profound and shocking ignorance, and it is reflected in every aspect of your society. And this is true, by the way, of all modern societies, whether market-based, socialist, developing, authoritarian, or imperial.

What Is to Be Done?

The first task is to name these processes, pick a socially generated fear, and work with it consciously. Practice naming the fear with as many people as you can. This will alert people to the processes that create fear where there is literally nothing to fear.

Second, help people track how the social and cultural processes generate and perpetuate fear; then help them see how that fear lodged within them festers, shapes priorities, limits choices, and constricts their full humanity. This work of discovery is frightening all by itself, and people require support as they learn to investigate this for themselves.

Third, teach people skills to respond to what they discover in themselves. Some simple Buddhist practices can be helpful, such as the practice of generating compassion for oneself. This reverses the prominent Western ethical teaching of putting others first; self-compassion is the essential first step. No one can give to another what she has not first given to herself.

Generating kindness and compassion for oneself and for one's own fearfulness calms and activates the heart. When the heart-center opens, the vicious cycle of fear and aggression or fear and greed can be interrupted. In sum: See it. Name it. Respond with compassion and kindness. That is all that is required. Everything else flows from it, like mountain streams to the sea.

Fear Creates Its Own World

When fear is contained and deconstructed, there can be an enormous release of energy. What do we mean by "deconstructed"? Fear is easily generated, and once given some form and shape through speech and action, it begins a life of its own. It seems to acquire intention and even personality, a more solid reality than its origins in the realm of subjective perception would justify. Fear begins to generate its own intention, strategy, tactics, allies, bargains, and calculations. It gathers up energy through the twinned processes of exaggeration and deception, swelling up like a great tick on the body politic. It settles in the lower chakras of individuals, erecting impenetrable barriers to thoughtful intelligence and heart-centered perception. Fear is *the* primary obstacle to the emergence of wisdom and compassion, and fear makes the integration of wisdom and compassion within the heart-center impossible. In fact, fear can block conscious access to the heart-center.

There are many consequences that flow from this, but the one we want to teach you about today is how it interrupts the flow of energy. At the level of the physical body, fear constricts the fluent movement of energy up and down the central channels of the body; this affects the chakra system, neural transmissions, the flow of chi, and the flow of oxygenated blood. An organism experiencing chronic fear will also experience many impaired bodily functions. Acute fear in response to a specific environmental challenge is a call to action, which the organism usually performs instantly. If the threat is averted, the acute fear drains away. The system returns to equilibrium. Not so with chronic fear.

Beyond the bodily level, fear also inhibits emotional and intellectual energy. To feel one's feelings should be simple enough for human beings, but it is astonishingly difficult in some cultures, including your own. Feelings are generally not accepted as valid evidence about reality, nor are most feelings considered legitimate motives for behavior. (Market pressures may urge people to follow their desires for pleasure or escape or release, but that is not the feeling life we are referring to here. The market place offers opportunities for masking difficult feelings, such as impotence, anxiety, or—yes, fearfulness.) A person drenched in fear cannot open up his or her heart to its source or to others.

Similarly, a person gripped by fear is unlikely to be able to assess the situation calmly, think outside the box, gather the relevant information, or imagine a creative solution. It is very difficult to think deeply and analyze a problem from several angles while awash with fear and anxiety. Good teachers, skillful negotiators, and wise people know this, but it is astonishing how rarely it is brought into public practice in your world.

There is more to say on a technical level about how chronic fear impedes the proper functioning of a person's energetic systems, from the dense physical body, the heart-center body, and the intellectual or cognitive body, to the more subtle levels of energy that shape receptivity to higher frequencies of energy and the subtle energies in other organisms. The important point, however, is simple: fear undermines the proper functioning of every organism at every level; chronic fear results in a stunted, ill, self-destructive organism. If that organism is as powerful as humans sometimes are, it can also fuel aggression and violence toward others.

We are looking now at a world built upon fear. It is uninhabitable, dysfunctional, and teetering on the edge of collapse. The heart-center must be restored to its central function as the source of both compassion and wisdom. The cultural values and practices accumulated around fear must be altered dramatically, before they undermine earthly life itself. As we have said before, this work must be done one person at a time. It does *not* require some moral conversion or ethical revolution. That has never been successful in human history, and it will certainly not be powerful enough now. It requires clear-eyed naming of what is, a pragmatic response to unveiled and demythologized reality. Humans are quite sturdy enough to bear the truth, and the truth is easy enough to speak: the fundamental reality of human life—indeed, of earthly life—is interdependence, not solitary individualism and competitiveness. It is the false belief in the latter, which gives rise to so much fear, and from fear arises the cascade of dysfunction, conflict, and frankly, stupidity in social and communal human life. The only antidote to this is life from the heart-center. This will be possible, one person at a time, as fear is named, deconstructed, and disabled. We will turn to that in the next chapter.

<figure>❂</figure>

VIII Dissolving Fear

This, then, becomes the work. You could now go to the blackboard and make a diagram of how all these topics are related and how one leads to the next; then you would want to take another piece of chalk and draw a great feedback loop. These are not linear processes but rather exceedingly complex nodes of interaction; each aspect is intimately connected to the others. There are linkages within single organisms, linkages between organisms on the same and different energetic levels, and links with the environment and other species. There are links beyond the human environments as well, which resonate with other kinds of energy fields and exhibit other communicative possibilities. Each of these links, some binary and some not, have feedback loops, which can intensify or undermine relationships. It is too complex for you to visualize.

That is no surprise, for we are actually crawling along the edges of an extraordinarily complex phenomenon that the wise ones have called "cosmic Mind," "the Creator," or the "big bang." Some day we will teach you that subtle knowledge, but not today. Today we wish to focus on how to undermine the reign of fear in your world.

Relieving humans of the reign of fear is the great work that will facilitate the great transformation. This will infuse your life work for the rest of your life. All who participate in this work must be attentive to their own habits of fearfulness. The work must proceed on several levels: with those who will in turn become skillful teachers of others; with those less conscious of how their own minds work, but who are still able to bring new skillfulness with fear into their work and their local communities; and with those for whom this will be their first opening to the larger dimensions of energy, interdependence, and global communities. Later we will help you map out a "curriculum" for meeting the needs of each group.

Four Steps to Dissolve Fear

One might choose many metaphors for this work: maturation, healing, consciousness raising, spiritual transformation, conversion, and awareness. We suggest, at least for now, relieving the burdens of living lives drenched with fear. Living with fear is an enormous burden; it imprisons individuals in cramped and desolate lives.

The first step is to help people name their fears, which is as challenging as helping fish name water. This can be accomplished through a therapeutic intervention—for example, the process of peeling back layer-by-layer behaviors, attitudes, and inner narratives until one finds the core issue, the deepest fear. In a discussion of personal difficulty, political grievance, global injustice, or any tension or conflict, one can ask questions until the experience of fear can surface and be recognized. Reframing a personal fear as an instance of the universal human experience of fear can provide a solvent for releasing an habitual denial. A dramatic opening is often the outcome, ripe for response.

To name a deep, strong emotion often begins to weaken its effects, and sometimes even disarms the source. The second step, after naming, is to stand still and try to interrupt the cascade of denials, resistances, defenses, and automatic inner narratives. To consciously experience the fear in one's body and mind, watching it flood every corner of your being, is a stunning experience for most people, especially the first time. The second step then is to identify the automatic, unskillful strategies of repression, deflection, and projection intended to quench the unpleasant experience of fear.

The third step follows immediately, if there really has been a full stop. One watches the fear; where does it go? How does it communicate its presence? How does it mobilize the body? How does it shut down parts of the mind and the self? How does it affect one's best self? One's least developed self? This third step initiates a lifetime of paying attention to oneself in new ways. Self-enquiry is one of the most powerful tools available to a human being for expanding awareness and opening the heart-center. It opens modes for communicating with others, in body and out of body, your species and other species. It is life-giving and life-enriching work. Learning how to teach it to others will engage you and many students around the world. You will find it deeply intriguing and rewarding. We will also help you to create forms to help support others in this work.

The fourth step is quite interesting: How must a person change her life as she becomes more aware of how fear has permeated her being? This too should be an ongoing process, with many steps of self-liberation. What is the fruit of relieving oneself of the burdens of fear? One might expect profound insights, explosions of creativity, increased integrity, more freedom in speech and action, richer communication on all planes, and dramatic openings in personal relationships.

Don't think that all relationships will become more loving and kind. That is not the case. Because much more truth can be expressed, some relationships will improve and others will collapse.

Brief Summary

We continue to speak of the second kind of fear, the imagined and habitual fearfulness, not the fear that gives useful information about a threat in the environment. Fear triggers a contraction of mind, heart, and body. This is exactly the opposite of what is needed to respond appropriately to the new surges of energy entering the earthly realms. This is a moment when all beings, but especially humans, can open to higher frequencies of energy, which will allow for more complex forms of communication, a richer understanding of personal and species interdependence, and ultimately, a great expansion in human consciousness and understanding. New levels of meaningfulness will be accessible.

All the energetic bodies of a human being must be able to open more, and fear inhibits that. Responding more skillfully to fear is essential for opening the heart-center, and only the heart-center can guide humans to live in ways that will not result in humanity's self-destruction. Identifying and dissolving fear is *the* essential work to save human life on the planet, to protect the precious life of the planet, and to continue the cosmos's great quest for self-conscious Mind. That seems compelling to us. Our task is to guide, support, and teach all who are able to take a responsible role in this essential work. It will inaugurate a new level of partnership between the largely invisible Teachers and the embodied students. We will also help you find each other, so you can create networks of people engaged in and committed to this work. It is revolutionary work, which you don't recognize yet. It will change the fundamental structure of human relationships and alter the need for and functioning of many human institutions.

Interlude: A Sense of Place

May I please pose a question? Listening last night to Barry Lopez, environmentalist and nature writer, I was suddenly struck that one way to dilute fear is to nourish our sense of place. When a community is grounded in a shared sense of place, is it better able to dilute the "reign of fear"?

That is an astute observation, which deserves further discussion. Let's begin this way: an immediate and far-reaching consequence of the hyper-individualism of your society, which we have discussed earlier, is that each person recognizes her isolation and consequent self-reliance. The underbelly of freedom, self-determination, and individual autonomy is a proportionate increase in a sense of personal vulnerability. A person may not actually be vulnerable, but she is a creature designed for life within a small group; her body, especially the lower chakras, recognizes her isolation and understands it as vulnerability. The fear that arises is not generated in her mind. Her fear is a response to the warning about her isolation and vulnerability.

People in your society are taught that the best response to such a sense of vulnerability is to improve one's competitiveness in whichever realm is at risk—personal survival, work, financial security, or family (the stand-in for intimate personal relationships). That only intensifies the underlying problem of isolation, the source of much dysfunction in your society, in both private and public life. It drives the addictive consumerism, superficiality, and heart-wrenching hungers of modern life.

You are quite right to see that reinforcing a sense of belonging to a local place, in association with others who also belong there, can begin to heal that sense of exposure and insecurity, which gives rise to so much diffuse fear and anxiety. How can this be accomplished? One begins by helping people to choose to remain in one place long enough to put down roots, as one says so wisely in English. One must know not only where the Laundromat and the best service station are, but the important features of the landscape and when the trees leaf out in the spring. Knowing where one's drinking water comes from and where one's garbage goes helps create a mental map of one's life on the land. Finding favorite places to walk, recognizing certain trees, and understanding the arrivals and departures of the migrants—insects, birds, and mammals—all help to ground one's sensibility in one's own neighborhood. Watching how other species grow, reproduce, and then die settles some human confusion about the shape and destiny of a life in body. All this can prepare the mental and emotional ground to join with others to protect a wetland or support local agriculture. Any activity on behalf of one's own neighborhood deepens one's rootedness in it and one's sense of belonging within a particular place and landscape.

Belonging to a caring community is the best antidote to the fears that arise from rootlessness and vulnerability to forces beyond one's control, from bad weather to bad labor markets. There is little harm from weakening one's ties to the national and global structures so disconnected from local life, for that can inoculate against some of the worst consequences of hyper-modernity. Global markets in particular have a very deleterious effect on many, directly or indirectly. Anything that provides an exit from a global market is likely to improve the true quality of life, from helping major chakras to relax into equilibrium to improving the quality of food and increasing the transparency of political decision making.

Such a return to the local can be a highly effective way to reduce the chronic fear of so many contemporary people, for they are intimately connected. These huge organizations and institutions, impersonal and impervious, stimulate anxiety and fear. People can identify their fears of globalization, unemployment, poisoned water and depleted land, poor quality food, and infringements of their fundamental humanity. It is more difficult to identify their more personal fears of loneliness, insecurity, illness, and death. The realms of fear are linked, and fear of the global system can give access to inner fears; then, healing and growth are possible.

The basic four steps we discussed earlier are useful in this context as well. Local organizations or small groups can adapt them to fit their own concerns and goals. Communities too can work with fear. It helps to release energy, achieve better responsiveness, and discover creative solutions to long-standing problems. Such group work can support the courageous individual work of its members as well.

Fear Is the Mortar of Public Institutions

Where there is fear, there is always power. The exercise of power generates fear in others. The experience of fear releases the desire for power. Once this cycle is generated in any human relationship, human life becomes very complicated. Finding one's way back from this vicious cycle challenges the most awake and skillful. Fear and then power become the mortar of social and political institutions. Brick-by-brick habits of relating accumulate, until certain patterns are so routine and habitual they take on the robes of sacred laws and inviolate traditions. Peer under the robes and peel back some of the verbal dressing, and you will find fear and power in their deathly dance.

Walk down any village street or through any city center and you will see nothing but evidence of this accretion of human fear and the desire for power. Every modern building is a physical manifestation of the ancient duo, fear and power. The fear of the intruder and the stranger manifests in gates and locks. The fear of the other eventually manifests as customs offices and police stations. The fear of want manifests as shops and stores and banks. The fear of disorder manifests as traffic lights, insurance companies, and policemen walking the beat. Look at this world with curiosity, and the deeper meanings of old structures will reveal themselves to you.

The more power, the more fear. In many ways, Hobbes was right, but he stopped too soon in his analysis of human fearfulness. He uses human fear to justify the exercise of unlimited sovereign power, admittedly an effective solution to widespread insecurity, but only in the short term. He looked in the wrong direction. The problem is not to use authority, force, and institutional violence to guarantee the security of the citizens, but rather to quench that insecurity at its very roots.

That is what our project is about. We have circled 'round and 'round the phenomenon of human fear in our desire to teach you to study it deeply. Then hopefully you will understand that your society (and most others) has pursued the path of self-medication to deal with the consequences of that fear. The more skillful path would be to address the fear directly and to recognize its location in the human heart.

Fear and Greed

The relation between fear and greed must be quite similar to those between fear and power and fear and the exercise of force.

Yes, indeed. For greed shows as well as any X-ray the deep fear of want in someone's heart. Greed manifests itself in economic institutions and regulations, and perhaps most clearly in market-based behavior. Those particular patterns of behavior make a market. No market really exists apart from the behavior related to buying and selling, and no one buys or sells or enters a market except to harvest some gain. Trading or buying and selling in the market place for food, shelter, and other necessities also flows from fear, but it is the functional fear, which recognizes information critical for survival (and not the imagined fear we have been discussing). As there are two kinds of fear, so are there two kinds of market activity. It is easy to tell the difference. In the first, once the need is satisfied, the person leaves the marketplace. In the second, the need cannot be satisfied, as it is produced in the mind, and so the person cannot leave the marketplace. In extreme cases, some kinds of market behavior can become addictive.

These market behaviors can become habits, first of individuals, and eventually, of so many people that they create institutions, laws, regulations, and standards. Some practices are legal, and some not. Some are more efficient than others. Some require certain skills; law schools, business schools, and economic institutes emerge. A whole network of institutions and institutional practices develops to shape and reproduce certain fear-driven practices. Look at your society to see what we mean.

Fear and Politics

What you describe is surely also true for political institutions—monarchs, legislatures, and courts.

Yes, of course. Establishing predictability in human behavior and enforcing consequences for those who do not comply is the institutionalization of the rule of law. Although those institutions are a direct manifestation of your ancestors' fears of disorder, they actually do function, at least in part, as their designers intended. It is largely their ability to enforce consequences (police, courts, prisons) through fear that reduces the insecurity of the larger society. Fear is used to control people's behavior, the oldest motivation of all. It surely is effective in many situations, though not all, and not without significant cost.

That is Hobbes's dilemma. Great fear is used to control great fear. There has been no increase in freedom or consciousness or even humanity. The political realm has focused and redistributed fear, but it has not banished fear, nor made it any less potent as the fundamental determinant of human behavior and even human experience.

Another route must be found. Plunge into that primal fear—not out on the street or in the world—but inside, into the very depths of your own human heart. Fear sits in the human heart sucking out the marrow of human possibility, of the gifts of relatedness, communicativeness, kindness, and ease. It is only in the human heart that fear can be softened and released. Only then will it be possible to address the institutions, the political practices, and the cultural values that so enshrine your collective fearfulness. You cannot recreate your society until you have released yourself from those obstacles in your own being; then you can address the fears of your society's founders, which led to the construction of your society as it is now. This is the great work now; this is the challenge from the world of Spirit. It is also the most radical work imaginable, for when you are free of your unconscious fear, you are free indeed. This is the work of healing the heart and allowing the heart-center to speak aloud.

IX From Fear to Wholeness

The Necessity of Colleagues

We return now to our starting point: this is a moment of great transformation, in fact literally cosmic transformation. Significant shifts in the energy arriving on earth are creating profound challenges for human beings; some can adjust to the new frequencies and intensities of energy, and some cannot. The subtle equilibrium among species and ecological regions has been disturbed, some aspects profoundly so. Rebalancing the many life forms on the planet will be the work of the next century, and while it will require the conscious work of the global community, it will largely be accomplished through the innumerable small adjustments every living being makes to environmental disturbance and disruption.

This is very difficult for people to understand, we have learned. The appropriate human responses must occur on every level: conscious and unconscious, material, psychic, emotional, intellectual, individual, group, state, and global. How can this be taught so human responses can be appropriate, timely, and fruitful?

Fortunately, there are countless embodied beings such as yourself turning to the task. The more complex the mind and the deeper the understanding, the better able someone is to recognize the many dimensions of this work and hold them, literally, in mind. This can be overwhelming and even lead to depression and suicide. That is tragic. People must remember there are many others working on the same great turning. Colleagues are not what is missing. What is missing is your awareness of each other. Then you can build cooperative networks—sometimes simply to communicate and share insights and information, and sometimes to organize sustained action together. Such collaborative efforts are vastly more effective; they are a perfect example of how the whole is much greater than the sum of its parts. Energy is generated, sustained, and directed to a particular point of leverage. When that point is activated, more energy is released, and the group can turn to the next task, reinvigorated and encouraged. This is what we will discuss in this chapter.

Because fear is both the proximate and distal cause of most dysfunctional and destructive human behavior, the most important task is to make the fear conscious and then to address it in deep and powerful ways. This is always ongoing work, both within and between people. Everything human can be addressed in this manner: identify the root fear and then address it consciously and skillfully.

Creating Community

There are many medicines for fear: cognitive, linguistic, conceptual, sensual, emotional, psychic, spiritual, social, and political. Although we are nearing the end of this book, we will, if you are willing, offer you more teaching texts, which will address various fears and their proper antidote. Each remedy, if applied appropriately, can eventually reach the heart-center. As the heart-center softens and opens, it loses its self-protective self-isolation. The healing and healed heart begins to look for colleagues, for partners in its work in the world. As it experiences its own ease, kindness, and insight, it naturally wishes to connect with other such hearts and beings traveling similar pathways. It will seek community, not in the old way of seeing its weaknesses and miseries mirrored in the lives and faces of others but in a new way. It wishes to gather with other centers of compassionate and healing energy, that they might reinforce each other and become stronger, more potent, and more adept. Building community is *not* an "ought," not some simple tactical necessity, but a natural, organic expression of a deeper reality. The healing heart recognizes its interdependence with all beings, and the emergence of community in many forms is a natural expression of that recognition. The emergence of such community cannot be interrupted or thwarted. If it is not present on one level, it will be found on another. If it has no social reality, at one moment, it will be found on a psychic or spiritual level. The beings will gather; the heart-centers will recognize there is no fundamental separation. There can be no absolute experience of isolation. Separation is recognized as an error arising from ignorance, and nothing more.

You might ask, how can these people, gathered or not gathered but connected in some way, impact the world? That is always the question of those who see what could be, if only.... This takes us back to our earlier teachings about the nature of mind and the immediate impulse of the great change now at hand.

Here is a simple image, not altogether perfect, but useful for the point. Imagine each awakening person as a tiny stream high on a mountainside. It runs its course, imagining three things: that it is the only stream, that it is choosing to go where it is going, and that it is accomplishing its heroic passage through its own effort and skill. It meets first one and then more such little streams, each with the same, shall we say uninformed understanding of reality? It rests a while in a small pond and sees with some relief this must be where it really belongs, for so many other little streams have gathered here as well. Life is different, but it seems to be predictable and safe again. Soon, however, the little stream heads down the mountainside again, part of a mightier river than ever it had known before. It is not so sure anymore that it is choosing its own route, though the speed is exciting; surely this is a remarkable achievement of its very own! Imagine this process repeated many times over, each race downward to a new plateau shifts the dominant self-understanding, eroding the sense of particularity and specialness, and making it increasingly clear it is participating in something large and powerful. Little is under its own control. Little mind gains in insight as it loses what it in truth never had had—a belief its own autonomy and its importance in the larger scheme of things.

The point is clear: it is as natural as succumbing to gravity. When people volunteer for this most significant work in the world, they find their community of like-hearted fellow volunteers. Their energies joined, they pause in their coming together, and then they continue the journey, gathering up more and more energy and momentum.

How might we say this in the language of energy and mind? As we explained earlier, each being, and most especially each human being, is an expression of universal Mind, of Mind as source and vehicle of consciousness. The fundamental reality of life itself, in an ontological sense, is that no being is separate from any other; each fully participates in the fullness of big Mind. Each little stream is simply water in a particular form, but all streams are water. Likewise, each little mind is Mind in a particular form, and all minds are nothing other than Mind. The obstacles to recognizing this simple fact, for it is a fact, have absorbed humans for eons, a phenomenon which has long entertained the Teachers. It is the history of human fearfulness. As fears are addressed skillfully and hearts open, the obstacles to recognizing this fact of oneness (a word we dislike heartily), of non-separation and non-isolation, also dissolve. At one level, this is not such a big deal. How could recognizing such a simple fact be so earth shattering? But it is. The world's religious traditions and practices offer roadmaps to the trailhead of this recognition. Those who follow the trail at a propitious moment in their own soul's development will discover it. They will then, as the Zen tradition teaches so memorably, recognize again that the mountain is the mountain and the stream is the stream. Nothing is changed, and everything is changed. It is all in the seeing. There is no separation; there is only interdependence. The healed and open heart relaxes into heart-mind, and then the teaching can begin.

It is so simple it defies logic. You wonder, how could you even tell someone about this, when it is so obvious, so absurdly clear? You don't even know how to describe your own discovery of it, it has been so subtle. Why would anyone, ripe in their own development, need intensive instruction to discover this simple fact? That is the sweet, beguiling mystery of human beings, but thus it is.

So the gathering of the beings embodies the truth of non-separation and interdependence. That in turn further opens the heart, and the being can relax on every energetic level. This allows a more skillful focus on the new frequencies of energy. Put more simply: as a chakra opens, especially the central chakra of the heart, more and higher frequencies of energy can be received. The chakras receive and process energy; the higher chakras are antennae reaching far out from the physical body, tuning in to energies rarely available before. That is the teaching. It describes the profound changes you have experienced these last years. Now we can connect the dots and show the linkages from heart-opening and creating community to more skillful receptivity and responsiveness to the new frequencies of energy arriving into the human and earthly realms.

Interlude: A Student's Gratitude

Good morning, great teacher. I have just reread this moving and exciting section. Perhaps I am beginning to take in some of this stunning teaching. I am so grateful to be allowed to receive it. Please help me surrender more fully to this process and work.

This is necessarily a gradual process. Otherwise, a sudden infusion of our powerful energy could lead to psychological or physical breakdown. The heart and brain can only process so much at a time, and each must be awakened and stretched gradually. It is more like physical exercise, than perhaps you realize. If you haven't been active for a while and then try to climb a mountain, you will surely be stiff and sore, if you manage it at all, and there is always danger of major injury. We certainly intend to avoid injury, because we wish to nurture your own growth and well-being. We Teachers are very protective of our students; without them we would have much less access to human lives. Dreams are a slow way for us to work, and they leave so much to interpretation. We much prefer this kind of communication.

That is very interesting. May I ask another question? The last time we spoke, you said you dislike the word "oneness." Would you please explain why? I sense there might be an important teaching there as well.

Yes, of course. The trouble with "oneness" as a concept, beyond the trouble with all concepts, which reify processes and experiences more subtle and fluid than conceptualization usually suggests, is largely in how the word is used. Too frequently it refers to something that is more accurately described as an "undifferentiated aggregate." Jung's use of "participation mystique," which he borrowed from a school of anthropology, also refers to that phenomenon. Psychologists recognize a certain kind of merging between beings, which doesn't transcend differentiation, but precedes it, chronologically or developmentally. People can be so fully identified with and immersed in a group, for example, that there is little capacity for individual consciousness or action. This is perhaps *the* major hindrance to awakening among humans right now. And what sustains that immersion in the group is deep and learned fear. Learning to fear the group's enemies reinforces one's identification with the group, and that in turn increases one's willingness to subordinate oneself to the group. Nearly without exception, that is psychological regression, an instance of reverse development. This is why people whose soul's development could allow them to deepen their consciousness neglect to take advantage of that propitious moment. They choose, because of fear, to remain enclosed within their group—often an extended family, kinship system, or political community. This is what "oneness" really means. It refers to those situations where there is little individual self-awareness, because the individual is submerged in a group identity. We might add here, though it is a different topic, that one also tends to find hierarchical power structures in such groups, for the same reason. Individuality (not individualism, which is the ideology valuing hyper-individuality) is essential for equitable horizontal relationships, power sharing, and what you would consider democratic and egalitarian processes.

Individuality, being one's own person, is an essential step to waking up. It is unavoidable, nearly true by definition. The kind of community we talk about is not characterized by oneness. It is the coming together of conscious beings aware of themselves and able to come into conscious relationship with each other. Such communities are drawn together primarily on psychological and subtle levels, rather than forming around some putative shared identity such as ethnicity or place. Bonds and obligations are reciprocal and voluntary and do not interfere with anyone's development. The core of the community is discovering the shared path; then energies are gathered and focused to pursue a shared goal and purpose. There is great freedom here, unlike a situation characterized by oneness.

Let us turn to the second word of this section: wholeness. This too is tricky in your culture, because of its profound misunderstanding of self and other. People experience such devastating degrees of isolation and separation, that many are mentally and psychically ill. The hunger for healing is great, but the forms available are inadequate. People longing for healing settle for oneness; they immerse themselves in some collective form, such as popular culture, mass media, or populist regressive politics. Even violence is a misguided attempt to relieve people's painful isolation.

The medicine for the acute sickness of contemporary society is the experience of wholeness. The instinct is not the problem. The problem is the false promises about how to achieve it. The only reliable healing is for each person to find wholeness within herself or himself. Contemplative communities, monastic life, and extended retreats can provide settings for this. But we wish to address your society as it is right now. Finding inner wholeness opens a person's heart to the unseen, the non-material, and the realm of Spirit. That opening and softening leads to healing and growth; she begins to recognize what is meaningful to her. Then she can discover her purpose in her life and world. It radically reframes what it means to be a human person.

Beginning to experience wholeness and completeness makes relationship with Spirit possible. If "relationship with Spirit" is too—what shall we say, partisan?—say instead some glimpses into big Mind and the deep interconnectedness of all beings. Such a person then can recognize the fundamental structures of interdependence. Deep relief and healing follow. In a sentence, interdependence and freedom are both essential, and together they give rise to community.

Interdependence

What does interdependence really mean, when we say it is a fundamental characteristic of reality? A Westerner like you might hear the "dependence" part of the word, and retreat a bit. In your culture, it suggests vulnerability, incompleteness, or even immaturity. Those connotations are only accurate from the point of view of ego, of little-self. After all, the major self-assigned task of ego is to demonstrate it is indispensable. Try to put all those associations aside, as we speak of a deeper meaning of the word.

We understand interdependence to mean all embodied life is a single system, indescribably complex, of course, but with identifiable patterns, processes, and energetic rhythms. There is no life outside that system. The word "system" means, by definition, that all parts are interdependent, and that any change in one component of the system causes change in other components. That is actually how one identifies the boundary of a system. Food cycles, for example, reflect the complex exchange of energies within a system; adjacent parts are closely linked, and more distant parts are less tightly linked. All energy systems—for example temperature, atmospheric pressure, and chemical reactions—work this way. It is also true of the human energy bodies—emotional, mental, and spiritual. The developing human capacity to receive higher frequencies of energy, the theme of this project, will impact all energy bodies, because each human being is an integrated system. Similarly each human being is a functional component of larger systems. Life is living systems enclosed within multiple living systems.

This is what we mean by interdependence. If we could find a stronger word, we would use it. We need a word that expresses inter-structural necessity way beyond the child's dependence upon the parent for nourishment and protection. We are pointing to levels of structural connection, which are invisible, in part because they are ubiquitous. Again, we are speaking of water to fish. Perhaps some examples would help: a slight change in planetary temperature could make life impossible for many species. A slight wobble in the earth's orbit could provoke such a temperature change, but so could human crowding into huge energy-using conglomerates (think of cities spewing out carbon dioxide). An organism lodged in an animal's gut escapes and finds a hospitable environment in another animal gut, provoking a global pandemic of a disease deadly to humans.

Life has always been a single system. Now, however, human beings have the capacity to recognize that. This is new. Never before has the human mind been able to recognize the extent to which it is embedded in a single system. Contemporary computer technology allows you to model extraordinarily complex systems, and to recognize that the earth too is such a system. *The* major consequence of what you call globalization will be humans finally realizing this.

Globalization as a Metaphor of Living Interdependence

For years you have been thinking about globalization, especially as a set of interlocking political, economic, and social processes. You are correct to identify globalization and the rapid deterioration of ecosystems around the world as the major challenges to human life now. Globalization is the marker of much more significant processes underway, but which are less visible to humans. We see globalization as the sum of all the processes, which make the fact of global interdependence and universal structural relatedness visible and comprehensible to more and more people. By participating in global markets, global environmental work, global NGOs, global politics, global communications, and the Internet and worldwide web, people discover they are inescapably linked to others worldwide. They also realize, one by one, each in their own domain (sports, religion, arts, politics, science, social justice, environmental protection, etc.) that they are in fact neither autonomous nor separate.

Those who have been thoroughly acculturated to believe in individual autonomy with the right to pursue their own personal goals discover that this is at best a fervent hope. It can no longer be the value underlying life planning, much less as the criterion for public policy. Some of the striking failures of American domestic and foreign policy stem from this profound misreading of social reality. Autonomous individuals do not exist. Building government policies as if all citizens are autonomous individuals is simply foolish. It is no wonder so few programs and public policies actually work as predicted. It is surely not the fault of the intended targets of those policies.

We don't know of a historical moment when the "freelancer" really was a common social type, but it is certainly not a viable model today. It is an inaccurate picture of human reality. Science has far too long studied individuals. Studying relationships is admittedly more difficult, but it would certainly be more fruitful. Otherwise, new research findings will continue to mislead, rather than shed light on real social processes. (Ironically, space travel may offer an opportunity to learn more, for so much of the human environment must be recreated.) Only the study of systems embedded within systems will provide useful insights for people in this century.

At this historical moment, globalization is the dominant image of wholeness and of a fully inclusive human society. Can that image be understood at several levels at once? Perhaps. But one must be scrupulous about keeping the various levels clear. We do not wish to suggest, for example, that any one person can experience a greater degree of personal wholeness by participating in the global market place. It is much more complex than that. So hold this sentence in mind: globalization and consciousness are two aspects of wholeness.

Specialization and Modernity

Human beings have survived and flourished as a species because of their extraordinary ability to know something through its component parts. The divisions of knowledge have given your species unsurpassed adaptive advantages. Partial knowledge is the specialty of ego, of little and focused mind. Modern people are characterized by their mental specialization; most know a great deal about a narrow piece of reality. This is visible in the arts and sciences, in engineering and technology, in the structure of the labor market and the economy, and in the puzzling (to us) glorification of star athletes.

Many bemoan the fate of generalists in modern society, but the picture is actually a bit more complex. There is an unprecedented level of specialization in contemporary society. This only works if those small parts, each with his or her own narrowly focused specialty, can be fit into a larger whole, which then can function as a single system. This is usually possible, otherwise the "misfit" (note the word!) would be out of work and would either withdraw or retrain. The labor market makes this happen swiftly and often relentlessly.

But specialization also makes possible more complex human systems capable of more difficult tasks than any one person could manage. Though one might rail against the implications of specialization for each person's own development, it would be foolish to dismantle complex systems in order to reduce human specialization. Only a major catastrophe—epidemic disease, environmental collapse, or war—could turn back the processes of specialization. Before you wring your hands, let us suggest another possibility.

The Intelligence of Complex Systems

You and your contemporaries think of human beings as individual units; you rarely consider your communities and collectivities as having any primary reality except as an aggregate of those individuals. But that is just a habit of mind reflecting a deep premise of your culture. Start from the opposite premise, that the fundamental operating system is the collectivity and each individual is a component part. Then the division of labor and the development of specialization characterize a complex system. Each part depends upon the other specialized parts, which must be integrated into a single functioning whole. There needn't be any central planning office or authoritative intelligence directing this system; in fact, there is good evidence that central directives usually fail, and the system implodes in upon itself in some way. Rather, intelligence operates at the level of each component part, reflecting its knowledge of nearby operations. Communication emerges, and must emerge, from the initial division of labor, and communication increases as the complexity increases. So far, so good. This basic model can be used to understand many social organisms and behaviors, both human and non-human.

Globalization and Global Consciousness

This simple model also describes globalization. Specialization has increased to such an extent that now the composite system is truly global—not exhaustively global, which would mean nothing outside of it functions independently, which is certainly not true. But global nonetheless, in that connections continue to spread around the earth, and the depth of the interconnectedness grows with each passing day. Constituent parts of the emerging system are becoming increasingly aware of their interrelatedness, and all this is built upon divisions of labor. Global awareness follows the pathways of increased communication. More specialization in turn gives rise to more interdependence. More interdependence generates more communication, which in turn stimulates more awareness: of the other, of mutual relatedness, of interdependence in both power and vulnerability, between enemies and allies, and of near and far. The new system brings to the surface a new politics of shared and contested interests and vulnerabilities.

Those most knowledgeable about the world these days are fascinated by these processes of globalization and wonder about the implications for conventional structures of human behavior and relationships. But that is not the essential question. Globalization is only the epiphenomenal symptom, the visible grid, and the material impetus to the most important shift in human consciousness in a millennium. Global markets, global communications such as the Internet, and global movements of people, goods, and information stimulate new awareness of a simple fact: the interdependence of all beings.

Let us repeat the central point: all beings have lived in an interdependent system. Always. What is changing is that people now live in systems so complex and with such a global reach that many are becoming profoundly aware of their interdependence. They recognize that they are inextricably embedded in multiple interrelated systems, and that they could not survive one minute outside of that complex. It is one thing to be in such a world. It is quite another to recognize it. The next step will be to act on that knowledge, which will mean individuals will now have to learn to protect themselves by protecting the larger whole, and to assure their own individual flourishing by serving the well-being of the whole system.

This will require major efforts. We wish to mention two at this point: the first returns us to our discussion of fear. Fear is the major obstacle to the smooth expansion of such awareness. The second is reliable knowledge about what in fact serves the well-being of the system. One might think— oh, yes, that is the role of science. Well, yes and no, and not exactly the way science is constituted today.

A Brief Counterpoint: Fear Drives All Politics

You speak of politics within these complex systems of interdependence. Yet you also have taught that politics reflects fear. How do these two points of view come together, and how is fear to be managed within a system of interdependence?

Yes, indeed. These are difficult questions. If a central theme of this project is fear, consciousness, and the reality of interdependence, then its title could be that very phrase: fear drives all politics. Political life is most vibrant at the midlevel between the realm of isolated individuals, on one hand, and the emergence of global interdependence and consciousness, on the other. Politics is the ultimate tool for creating the other, which is the first and most powerful response to personal and communal fears. In this way politics can be a vehicle for managing increasing specialization and complexity; it can also define the limits of cooperative interdependence.

We are nearing the end of this project, though there is certainly much more we could say about many of the topics we have touched upon. There will be ample opportunities later to pursue some of these issues more deeply. Meanwhile, let me close this chapter with a suggestive list for you to consider.

- Politics is condensed fear.
- Evolution continues.
- What's so scary about interdependence?
- Individuality is not the end of human development.
- We need a science for the next century.
- The unused capacities of human beings is the great scandal of the twenty-first century.

- Moral exhortation is not the answer.
- It's what you can't see that matters.

I must say, beloved teacher, I love those statements. I so hope we can explore them some day.

X Starting Again

Teacher and Student Reflect on the Process

I 've been thinking about the eventual form of these teachings and how they might move out into the world. I hope you will help me with those big decisions, when it is time.

Of course, but it is not time yet. Do you have a question this morning?

I have been thinking about "bad spirits" since a recent conversation about channeling. Are there "bad" spirits that might take over a channel? Are there bad spirits at all? Is there an evil force in the universe? I have never thought so. What appears to us to be evil has often struck me as catastrophic ignorance or lack of development. But when I look long and hard at the Holocaust, for example, or the West's casual indifference to famine and genocide in other parts of the world, my arguments seem almost silly or academic. Would you teach us about that? What else you would like us to know? What is your agenda for us?

Good questions. Yes, there are many other topics we would like to discuss with you. Some will belong in the book that is emerging from these sessions. Some will go to another document, perhaps a second book. You could create a website for this material. There are more topics that are urgently needed in your communities now, and there are students and readers who would be well served by having access to our conversations. We would like to speak to you about spirituality and religion, for example. We would like to assist you to help the students find and connect with each other, and then to help them bring this new understanding to more and more people. We would like to tell you more about forms of social organization that would better meet people's needs and desires. We would like to say much more about consciousness, what that means, how it relates to common understandings of mind and mental phenomena, and how it can be expanded for people at various points of development. We realize you are not adequately informed about how karma functions, both for individuals and for communities.

At a later date, we would like to discuss forms of knowledge and knowing, and how scientific enquiry could be improved. We know you are very interested in education, and that you are profoundly disappointed with most educational institutions. We share that concern with you. Our main point is that the whole human world must be largely reimagined, if humans are not to destroy their livelihoods. Politics, schools, markets, families, and communities must take on new shapes for new tasks, if expanding consciousness is to be valued, as it must, as the next step in the human project. We would wish you to understand fear more deeply and then teach others about it.

As you see, there is plenty of work for us to do. Other teachers can join us as well. We recognize that this first project is by far the most difficult. Now you seem to have adjusted to the energy, but you still do not understand how you will shift from receiving these teachings to sending them out into the world. Please trust that we will guide the project, one step at a time, and that it will work smoothly. Gradually you will relax more deeply into the work, and we will turn to new topics, one by one.

That sounds wonderful. There is certainly a central theme in this project. Would you give me a title? It is labeled "new project" in my computer file.

(He laughs.) Well, it is hardly "new" anymore. What do you think is the major theme?

Consciousness. Interdependence. Fear as the fundamental obstacle to the expansion of consciousness and the recognition of interdependence. The cosmic shower of new energies with higher frequencies that stimulate a range of responses in all beings. This is a moment of transition and perhaps transformation, for which modernity, individualism, science, exploration, and the related social, economic, cultural, and psychological phenomena are all relevant, even necessary. This is about a profound shift in humans' relationship to Spirit, at the same time that it is post-religion, post-ethics, and post-materialism. This seems to summarize the main topics.

Very good! Do you think anything is missing?

Not really. It seems to be an analysis of the deep structure of human life, at this moment in human history. That sounds very grandiose, but it is something like that. It uses the notion of system to show the profound interconnectedness at every level of the planet, including all species and all energetic phenomena. The teaching reframes our everyday understanding of the major crises in our world, which invites a new interpretation of the world.

So, "reframing the world; reframing the human condition" captures some of that?

Certainly. And the reframing releases so much energy and confidence—or perhaps it is smarter to say dissolves so much fearfulness that new modes of behavior become possible. The shift in consciousness facilitates new forms of action and relationship. They might become, well, easy!

Precisely. We can see you grasp the major points. In your summary, you restate the teachings in your own words and make it your own. That was our hope. Now you can teach it to others.

My biggest concern is whether it will be comprehensible to people who do not recognize the availability of Spirit.

The entry point for them will be the critical concept of interdependence. Interdependence is obvious the moment one begins to look for it. The second entry point will be fear. Everyone recognizes fear, and everyone can recognize how fear underlies so much human behavior. Begin with interdependence or fear to open minds and hearts enough for a first step. There is no need to cover the entire journey; one step is enough. Someone else will point out the next step. Or not. Your task is to make the first step possible. No teacher ever has any more responsibility than that. Remember that.

Interdependence and fear are like a carrot and stick or the two poles of a battery. Enormous energy is generated between them; working with both is extraordinarily potent.

Fear and Interdependence

Fear and interdependence are two central aspects of globalization. Together they drive so much current politics; they may even provide the parameters of much contemporary social and political thought. Could it be that those focused more on fear would be relatively conservative and those who emphasize interdependence would be more progressive?

Those are certainly two different ways of envisioning the world, but they are not so separate; there are still points of contact and overlap. Some fear interdependence, for example, while others can manage their fear with their confidence in their interdependent relationships. Though the two concepts are enormously powerful, they are also tricky, and one must be alert about how and when to use them. We can say, however, that fear is fundamentally a construct of little-self, of ego-consciousness, and it reflects the thinking of an individual. This is not to ignore that fear is maintained and nourished by countless social and cultural practices, but individuals experience fear, either as diffused anxiety or intense emotion.

Interdependence, on the other hand, is a descriptive word that points to the realities of living organisms. Life *is* interdependent, and life is only possible if it is in equilibrium within essential systems. Interdependence is simply a fact, a different kind of concept than fear. We have been discussing the slow recognition of the fact of interdependence, which in turn serves to moderate fear; it softens boundaries and allows consciousness to expand and deepen. Eventually the boundaries become more porous, and the heart can open to the world.

Biological and ecological interdependence can be used as a metaphor for the more fundamental frame of interdependence, that of cosmic Mind. There is only a single Mind, from which all organisms and all forms emerge and from which they take their reality. This is perhaps too metaphysical for our purposes right now. Interdependence is the concretized interrelatedness whose source is Mind. A being's awareness of this indicates how conscious it is, and it will determine the being's experience of self and other, subject and object.

Fear, the opposite of attraction, is the most powerful isolating force in the cosmos. Recall our earlier distinction between the two types of fear: one grounded in immediate reality, functioning as a source of information, and one generated by imagination and sustained by narrative and language. Both take energetic forms, of course, but only the former is part of the structure of reality. The latter is fundamentally false or unreal because it has no energetic base, even though it profoundly impacts human life. Rooted in the human imagination, it obstructs human consciousness.

The Message and the Messenger

You would like to understand more fully the relationship between the message and the messenger, or why you must be transformed to better receive and digest the teachings. Your question can lead us to important problems, which you should understand.

Consider again our basic theme: humans are being bathed in new surges of energy, and the task at hand is to help as many as we can to receive this new higher-frequency energy. Then they will be better able to integrate the new energy and use it to create very different lives. Actually, all beings are receiving new energies, but for our purposes now we are focusing on how you and other students can be encouraged in this new work. We have discussed how fear is the fundamental obstacle to human receptivity to the energies of the cosmos and to the promptings and communication of Spirit.

It should not surprise you then that these are the same issues you face as you explore your own patterns and habitual responses. It is a beautiful example of an ancient wisdom: as above, so below. As the planet, so the person. In this teaching, we have addressed the levels of the planet and human communities, but everything is also vibrating at the level of the individual. Ocean and wave, river and water drop. Furthermore, and this may be a new idea for you, influence moves in both directions. The energies received by the planet impact each individual being; likewise, the energetic responses of each individual being can impact the community, the species, and the planet as a whole.

We have mostly discussed the first version of that equation, how individuals are impacted by planetary energies. Your question prompts us to look in the other direction. Every topic we have discussed so far is also reflected within your own psychic system. New energies, fears, obstacles, habits, and receptiveness are all available to you. Study your own experience. What is happening in your belly? How does your stamina ebb and flow? What are the phases of your mind's insights and enthusiasms? The intimate resonance between the micro and the macrocosmic levels can suggest insights into the lives of others as well as the subtle shifts for the entire human community. A warning though: it takes practice and disciplined discernment to navigate these multiple levels skillfully.

Your own capacity to receive, transform, and adapt to the new levels of energy will require constant upgrading and fine-tuning as you continue to receive our energy and teachings. You can think of this as being transformed into the shape and meaning of our message, so there is no gap between what you teach and who you are. This is a very high goal. It will enable you to teach from your core, not just from your intellect or mind. Then there is little danger of ego distorting the teaching.

Some students can only be channels; they are given the message and encouraged to pass it on. Even though it is more challenging, we hope that you will be able to embody and integrate the message more fully. This work is demanding, and we wish to support you in every way possible. Let me remind you: you are becoming the message. Your receptivity is essential; skillful responses to the new frequency of energy arriving from the cosmos are required of many now.

Wisdom and Compassion

It is crucial for you to understand that your current interior work is essential for your continued work with us. Please do not feel you are not doing what you should. Imagine our teaching sinking deep into your very being, into your emotional and physical bodies, such that you will be able to speak from deep within your own experience. This will shape your future work as a writer and teacher. Every step of this process is valuable, and we are making certain the necessary arrangements and support arrive at the right time. Think of this as wisdom made effective in real life; it reveals again the inseparability of wisdom and compassion, two aspects of a single way of being in the world. Wisdom without compassion is simply knowledge, and compassion without wisdom is simply reformism, or even less—"do-goodism." Intellectual knowledge is not wisdom; it is lifeless. Wisdom comes from understanding the full picture in the widest possible frame, and then being able to respond out of compassion. Only this releases ignorance and suffering.

Our teaching has been very intellectually stimulating for you. Your heart-center must be as open as your mind has been, so your new learning is wrapped in compassion. This is essential both for you and for all who will become students of this text. In that way, this will also be a compassion teaching, and its students will be able to receive the deep wisdom embedded in it. Your own understanding continues to deepen, revealing itself in your own teaching; your students recognize your compassion for them, which invites them to open to your teaching. We teach this way as well.

You have been unable to recognize fully our compassion and deep care for your well-being, and so listening to us has been unnecessarily strenuous. Please meditate on this and consider its implications. Unless you can also receive our compassion for you, our work will be truncated. To receive our compassion, the receptors in your chakras must be wide open and trusting. And so we return to fear. You too must tend to the old habits of fear buried deep in your psyche. We will support you as you identify the fears, rooted in lifelong habits.

Remember the four steps of your practice: see the fear and name it. Wrap it with compassion. And then recognize how you are also held in our compassion. Letting go happens nearly by itself, for the fear simply dissolves. It is a life practice.

◎

XI | On Love

Your main themes have been fear, interdependence, and consciousness. Where does love fit in?

The Commons of the Human Heart

Love is central: love as energy, love as purpose, love as value, love as concept, and love as practice. It is the fundamental theme of Western spirituality, even when it is clouded over by the accretions of poor theology, rigid dogma, and inhumane practices. Love is always present, shining in itself and drawing people in, one by one. Love plays a different part in the East. One could write a wonderful book tracing the central themes: love in the West and wisdom in the East. I see you wonder, isn't that the miracle of friendship, that it can contain both? Yes.

We could teach you everything we wish you to know through the lens of love. We chose not to do so because your culture no longer understands love. It has drenched its fundamental, foundational principle with toxin, obscuring love's shining potency. Your culture replaced love with sexuality. Even desire is obscured, reduced to release or narcissistic gratification. The practices of gift, surrender, care, generosity, nurturance, and commitment are belittled. Reciprocity, mutuality, and the dissolution of the self/other divide have vanished from the public teachings and practices of your society. It is the profound sickness of your world and the basic cause of your environmental destruction and your social and economic ills. Love is the medicine, which could heal everything, every single dimension of your deathly illness.

We don't think teaching love to your world would help much; the incomprehension and resistance are too great. That is why we have chosen these other avenues. Your people know they are fearful, or can be led to see that more easily than their ignorance of love. Your people can be taught to recognize the consequences of their competitive individualism, and they can expand their awareness of their own interdependence more easily than they can exchange self and other or follow the deep ethics of their religious tradition. Probably no human community could generate sufficient confession, repentance, and forgiveness to heal your society of its violence and injustice. Focusing instead on expanding awareness without directly assaulting the ego and its fortresses and fantasies is a more fruitful way to proceed. Will it eventually lead to repentance? Hopefully, but for each person, at the correct moment.

Love is easy to put aside, to dismiss as belonging to another realm or historical moment. In this world, ruled by the ego and the marketplace, there is little space left for love. But fear, oh yes, we can certainly see the reality of fear. The teacher has found a tiny opening, and the skillful teacher will then know how to proceed. Our intention is to train you to be such a skillful teacher, able to touch the tiniest crack in the ferocious facade.

The Student's Anxiety: Where Will This Manuscript Go?

I have many worries about our work. There is so much here I don't understand. Allowing myself to trust this strange process challenges so many old assumptions. The deepest fear is that I won't be able to complete this project or bring it out into the world. That is where I have always gotten stuck with my writing. There is a near-panic in me about that and a withering sense of imminent failure.

Okay. Let's start at the beginning: this is a good moment for a review. This is our project, initiated and supported by the Teachers. We are profoundly grateful for your willingness to join us and to bring this very important teaching out into your world. Your responsibility has been to show up, to learn how to receive the material, and to write it down. You have performed beautifully. You have gone further, however, by agreeing to do the hard interior work that would enable you to receive deeper teachings. You are taking better care of yourself and opening up your deepest self with great courage and perseverance. That will bear visible fruit for our work, for your understanding of yourself in the world, and for your well-being.

We told you learning to work with us would take some time and that we would help you become fluent and at ease. You can see that has happened. You have been warmed by people's responses to the teachings, and you are beginning to meet others who are bringing similar material into the world. This will normalize the work, which will relieve your anxiety about your ability to bring it to fruition.

There will be no problem publishing this text. When it is time, we will lead you to a receptive editor. We will suggest ways to improve its clarity. Be candid about authorship: it should list you as the author, and in the preface, you will describe this process. Everyone who knows you will recognize your voice and see that the text has indeed come through your mind, your sensibility, and even your vocabulary. This is how it should be. You have found skillful ways to describe our working relationship to people with varying backgrounds, and we are sure you will do this with increasing authority and ease, all in due time.

Meanwhile, keep a regular schedule with us; take excellent care of yourself, both physically and emotionally; clear out more of the debris from your early conditioning; and watch for ways to share the teachings. When it is time to send it out into the world in a more formal way, you will be accustomed to sharing it, talking about it, and even teaching it. This too will proceed step by step, and you will hardly notice the enormous distances you cover. We know what we are doing, and we attend to your strengths and weaknesses, so we can heal them, work with them, and bring you new insight and depth.

Whether or not we are actively working with you, we are present in your daily life. Pauses have their own value. Ignore your old neurotic belief that you must be constantly active. It is only a hindrance now. One last thing: when you return to the college in the fall, we will make sure you have adequate time and energy to stay rooted in our work. We meant it when we said your psychic development must become your primary focus. Your job—demanding, challenging, and satisfying—must take second place.

Buddha and Jesus: Spirituality in the East and the West

To "put on the mind of Christ" or to "put on the mind of the Buddha" are one and the same. Each serves as a gateway into cosmic Mind or Heart. The name matters not. The gateways open on to the single reality where there is no duality, no separation, and no judgment. Beyond time and space, it is a way of seeing and being that allows the full flowering of human consciousness. The gateways are unimportant; one walks *through* a gate. Only terrible fear would make someone stand outside the gate and insist the gate itself is the goal. Remember the Buddha's story about the raft one uses to cross the river: once you have reached the other shore, you don't pick up the raft and carry it on your shoulders; you leave it on the riverbank. Use the Jesus and Buddha stories to build a raft. Then Christ-mind or Buddha-mind awaits across the river. The point is to cross the river from duality to non-duality, from fearfulness to ease, and from separation to interdependence. That is the whole and entire teaching. You have always known this; you brought that understanding in with you. This text and those that will follow are simply deeper explorations of that theme, the truth before which all other truths are partial.

We explained in our last session why we chose fear rather than love as our central image for your society. This might also be helpful. Fear and love are complementary. Jesus said, "Love casts out fear, and perfect love casts out all fear." How can one develop that love that casts out fear? Love penetrates all reality; it is the fundamental energy of the cosmos. Love reflects the universe's intention that there be something rather than nothing. The most fundamental fear is that there is in fact nothing, rather than something. This fear is born of the imagination; it is not the fear that delivers critical information about the environment to enhance survival.

As there are two kinds of fear, so there are two kinds of love. There is the love of the immediate and the personal—love for mate and offspring, for example, and the many extensions of that into love of "we" rather than "them." That love is anchored in attachment to self, just as the first type of fear supports survival. The second type of love is free of attachment, which releases it from duality. That love flows from awareness of interconnection, and it embraces what is. Expressed that way, you can see it echoes the East's understanding of wisdom. Westerners must wrestle with their fears to experience the second type of love (the early Christians named this distinction *eros/agape*). Easterners wrestle with ignorance in their pursuit of wisdom. The two paths ultimately converge.

The disadvantage of using fear as a contemporary spiritual teaching is people's resistance to admitting their fear; even though fear is a core experience, it is laced with discomfort and shame. Still, it is helpful because dissolving even a small amount can release great energy. Releasing fear stimulates courage in the heart, the perfect antidote to fear.

Circling the Mountain

We are studying a single reality. Imagine we are circling a great mountain, and you must describe each view. Standing there on the mountainside, however, you experience a totality—smells, light, slope, grasses, rocks, clouds, wind, everything. If you can provide multiple snapshots of mountain views, your reader can reassemble them. You offer her a destination and a map; then she too can stand on the mountain slope and experience the whole mountain.

The Power of Teaching about Fear

Let us return to the question of why we speak of fear, rather than love, when we approach your culture. To teach of love does not bring any relief from the pain and constriction, the unfreedom of fear. To teach of fear puts a powerful tool in the hands of the student for releasing suffering. Fear is the underlying cause of suffering, and the fear of suffering itself compounds those processes that fear instigates and reinforces. Fear generates the defenses, the forms of denial, the subterfuges and projections, and the refusals to recognize the true state of things. Fear inhibits loving-kindness, clouds the perception of the truth, and intensifies suffering. Fear is largely a creation of the mind of little-self, and this is a very good thing. It means fear can be weakened, diluted, disconnected, and eventually dissolved. It has no fundamental reality, as it is a product of the human mind. As we have taught you before, ego requires fear for its self-substantiation and to justify ego's imperial presence in consciousness. There is real juice here, real material to work with, which can penetrate the fog of ego-consciousness, mitigate suffering, and open up the heart-center.

The Difficulties of Teaching Love

To teach love is a quite different project. It would seem a more direct route to our ultimate goal, which is the most expansive consciousness possible. But we have learned it does not work well on the human plane. Or it only works

119

well with those few humans already very far along their spiritual paths, and they usually are receiving guidance from their own teachers at that point.

Look at Jesus's experience: "Love your neighbor as yourself." Practically no one understands that teaching because they have no idea what it might mean to love oneself. Even the advanced Buddhist practice of replacing self with other maintains the separation between subject and object. But Jesus was trying to point to the truth: that there is no separation between self and neighbor. The deep meaning of that sentence was quickly lost because it is so radical.

A further difficulty teaching about love is that an everyday person with the usual consciousness can easily say, "Oh, yes, I do love people. I donate to charity, and I am kind to the weak. My politics reflects my belief that the strong should help the poor and the unfit. I refrain from violence, and I care for my family. I try to be considerate of every one I work and live with." Is that what it means to be loving in this world? The focus is on outer behavior, without much attention to deep attitudes and values.

Consider how much more potent a teaching about fear would be. It forces the mind to go inward, first of all, and to try to peer into a dark cranny or two. Even the fear of excavating deep fear can be useful material to work with. Fear and thinking about fear challenges beliefs, premises, and habits of behavior. Skillful questioning pulls away the veil of self-delusion and reveals the little old man behind the green velvet curtain, trembling in his impotence. It reveals the false posturing of little-self, and it surfaces the private narratives endlessly repeated to shore up the fragile face of the self.

These are substantial obstacles to loving-kindness, and so, the work with fear is by far the most fruitful and powerful method for expanding consciousness and removing the obstacles to clarity and truthfulness. Recognizing the unreality of ego's claims is what frees the natural energy of love and kindness, for the profound truth of interdependence and the non-separation of beings then becomes apparent. This is what really shifts consciousness. When fear is stripped away, love remains. Love is the substantial reality; it is love that characterizes the fundamental energy of the cosmos.

Here is the great paradox, which becomes a stumbling block for many students. Only love can identify, confront, and heal fear. Only the healing power of love, which we usually call compassion, can dissolve the toxicity of fear. This is the essential path of spiritual development. It begins with a glimpse of being held in love and compassion from somewhere beyond the constricted and fearful self. Then that self learns, probably through some form of halting imitation, to offer itself compassion for its own suffering and lack of freedom. Compassion and fearfulness struggle in a dialogue between two views of human life and the meaning of the great cosmic experiment of human consciousness.

Compassion and fearfulness have danced together all through human history, creating an energetic charge, which nearly defines human beings' great potential for consciousness and for recognizing who and what they are. If fearfulness leads to ever more darkness, then compassion turns on the lights. Compassion and fear are neither antagonists nor enemies. Compassion is triggered by witnessing fearfulness, and compassion can disarm and embrace the fearfulness of others. When the dance goes on within a human heart, as it often does in those walking the path of consciousness, it can confuse a student trying to make a decision or determine a response. If she can remain conscious of the dance, she can learn a lot about old patterns and unconscious assumptions. Great advances are possible when compassion is directed toward oneself and its confusions and suffering.

The Truth Love Knows

What is love, really, except the desire that the other flourish? And what is fear, really, except the desire that one's own self might flourish amid the immediate uncertainty about whether that is likely? So fear and love are extremely closely related, arising from the same life force. They move in two different directions, of course, and that distinction between objects—self and other—is precisely the error of fear. There is no distinction at the heart of the matter; self and other are not separated and certainly are not in any zero-sum relationship. When it appears to be so, it is a signal that perception is limited to the material level, where energy is its most dense and least sensitive, and where little-mind is most vulnerable to the false formations of its surrounding culture and society. One has only to dig down a few layers to discover how shallow is little-mind's understanding of its real essence and its fundamental relationship with other beings. The further one goes into the depth of a human heart, the more clear it becomes. Light streams in from the cosmos, revealing the myriad connections among all forms of life: all human beings, all desires of the human heart, all great questions of the human mind, and all sufferings of the human body and spirit. The more one explores the commons of the human heart, the more ease; then there can be genuine relaxation into one's given life-form. There is enough separation so that relationship is interesting and often challenging, but not so much separation that relationship is impossible. Any glimpse of the whole sweeps out the debris of isolation, misery, and meaninglessness, which causes so much human suffering. The narratives of fear simply drop away, for they no longer serve the purpose of shoring up the tiny, frightened little-self; there is no need. And when the narratives of fear and the fear of fear drop away, what is left? The heartfelt desire that every being flourish. In other words, love. Loving-kindness. And compassion.

The story seems so simple that even a child could learn it. And indeed it is true a child can learn it, for children are closer to their original knowledge of it. It is not so fanciful to say adult learning is really a forgetting of this most precious truth; nor is it fanciful to say that unlearning that adult thinking can help reestablish a truthful way of understanding life. One can preach and teach these ideas over and over; some might even come to agree with you. But it remains knowledge of the cognitive mind. But the experience is what is critical and that, as you have learned this season, is much more challenging. How to experience the entrenched nature and depth of your fears? How to unravel the old dense patterns, which prevent new knowledge and experience from penetrating? How shall you rename the realities you believe you see? How can you free yourself from the automatic responses to stimuli you don't even remember anymore?

From Simple Teaching to the Transformation of Consciousness

What could be deeper or more intense? What could be more potent or more radical? It all depends on your receptivity and the categories and metaphors that you are most comfortable with. The teaching is, in the end, simple. Now you can express it in short, clear sentences. The issue is not the teaching, sadly. For the teaching is timeless—ancient and modern, clear, and with a ring of familiarity. The real issue is how to move the teaching from a straightforward idea to a compelling reality in a human heart, a group, a society, a planet. That is our task and challenge now. Nothing is more essential for cosmic development. Its speed is measured by the parameters it must transcend.

One of those parameters is the future survival of human beings at a level of abundance that allows the continuing development of consciousness. Another parameter is the flourishing of the environmental systems necessary for human life. These two sentences refer to the same reality. Do we know, or is it ordained, that human and planetary biological life will continue to support the vast expansion of consciousness now possible? No. Unfortunately, for we too would like to know that. The big question now is not about the content of the teaching, but rather how we might spread the teaching further and faster. Perhaps even more urgent is to help people grasp the teaching at its deepest level, at the level of profound consciousness from which behavior, attitudes, and decisions arise. You have focused on the teaching, wishing to absorb it and integrate it into your map of the world and human reality. Now you want to know, what do we do now?

How to Become the Skillful Teacher

We want you to focus on how to help others grasp the teaching as the radical framework it really is. It is time to shift from receiving the message to becoming its teacher. You must learn how to help people dismantle the obstacles that obscure this shining reality. Before people can experience "the commons of the human heart," they must dive deeply into their own fears and unconsciousness, which deny them access to so much life-giving energy and delight. People can only free themselves from their fears; no one can do that for anyone. The labor is enormous, as you now well know. To free yourself from fear is actually to free yourself, the magnificent human work of self-liberation. Only a free person can love, recognize the interdependence of all beings, and live the reality of non-separation.

How can you become such a teacher? How can you develop the skills to assist others to dismantle their own structures of fearfulness? There are a thousand approaches to this work, or a thousand thousand. Each teacher will find his or her own way. We hope you will find this intriguing and that you will begin to experiment with different approaches. But whatever the form, with individuals or groups, don't confine yourself to your thinking self; it will not be as effective as the deep intuition arising from your heart. Language and action arising from your heart-center will be more potent than what arises from your intellect. You will recognize how differently these two centers respond in certain moments. There is no blame in responding from your intellect, but when the heart-center can also participate, it is much more powerful. Please let this teaching ripen; it is a seed that can bear much fruit.

Please remember your main task is to continue to strip out the old patterns that inhibit and imprison you. These spacious days and weeks are precious. Let yourself be as introverted and self-reflective as you wish, for it is those flashes of self-intuition that undo so many old sources of suffering. Please do not be anxious about the pace of our work; all is well. You need only to receive it as we bring it to you.

Before we finish, there is one more theme about love I wish to give you, and then there are a few more comments about how to teach this material, help it move into the world, and actually begin to change people's experience of their own fearfulness. You ask about editing this text. You may certainly tighten up this first version and remove the unnecessary phrases that can obscure rather than clarify the meaning. Please keep one copy of the original, verbatim version. At some point it might be helpful for someone to be able to see our actual process; those asides reveal another dimension of the process.

You also ask about your work at the college. You must remember one thing: the energy of this process in general and with this project in particular is very powerful. It *will* accomplish what it intends. And "will" is emphasized. Once your powerful patterns of old conditioning are dissolved, and that is happening as rapidly as the snow melts outside, our energy will flow through you easily. The college and its expectations of you will be unable to obstruct your desire to be in relationship with us and to be of use for this great transformation of consciousness that is underway. All that is required is your clarity. The "winter work," as you call it, has cleared out much old debris in your system. What remains will be released in the near future. Your clear voice speaking from your integrated heart and mind will take its seat, find its cadence, and claim its authority. Your ability to name what you perceive and to express it in fluent language will rise up from your lower chakras with all the strength and authority of a tribal leader. You will recognize your purpose here in this life, and everything else will be subordinated to it. All this will bring you profound joy. When will all this emerge? Very soon. The primary focus is still on your interior clearing, and then, you must build up your physical strength and your emotional transparency. Transparency? Perhaps not the right word. You will become conscious of your groundedness in relationship, in a way that expresses your own emotional truth and liveliness. You will become transparent to yourself and then to others.

One Chooses to Love

Now, one last piece on love. One must choose to love, and to love is a decision. To love is to lean toward the well-being of the other. This is not about romance or attachment or erotic desire, though each can be a school of love. Love is activity; love is a verb, not a feeling. There are not so many humans who love, and certainly not all who believe they love truly love. To love requires a certain degree of consciousness, and most humans are beginners. This is why we, the Teachers, have made certain strategic decisions. We adjust our teachings to the student's level of awareness. You too must learn to do that skillfully. Second, we focus on removing obstacles to the natural opening of awareness, because that is—perhaps counter-intuitively—the most direct method. And third, for most humans, identifying their fears and understanding how fear shapes their behavior and beliefs is a powerful way to dissolve the impediments to wider consciousness.

Fear makes clear decision making nearly impossible, for it blocks relevant information, constricts choices, and falsifies alternatives. It is no surprise that so many human projects self-destruct because they are based on ignorance and self-delusion and are organized by the misinformed and exaggerating little-mind. Calculations of self-interest are generally way off the mark. The whole project of reinforcing and defending an isolated little-self is destined to fail, because its premises are incorrect.

Choosing to love arises out of a person at peace with himself, whose interior conflicts have been resolved. Before that, various parts of the self war with each other over what is real, what is necessary, and what would be preferable if it could be accommodated. An enormous amount of psychic energy is consumed in these intrapersonal arguments. Each part of the personality must be carefully heard, wrapped in compassion, and then gradually integrated into the whole. This is the meaning of "integrity." When split-off pieces have been brought back into the orbit of consciousness, when heart and mind centers are in easy relationship with each other, and when desire and obligation are reunited, then the integrated person can choose to love.

This brings us back to our starting point. We have circled the mountain. You can call it truth, love, the growth of consciousness, or human responses to the new energy arriving within the orbit of your planet. You can speak of the great shift underway or the terrifying problems of planetary destruction because of a runaway economic system. You can describe the dangers of markets penetrating deep into arenas where other forms of decision making are much more appropriate, or you can focus on the hyper-individualism of contemporary culture and how that impedes your ability as a species to live in environmental and biological balance. You can discuss the hunger for Spirit in so many human hearts, perhaps unprecedented in human history, or the inability of the major religious traditions to meet that hunger or respond to the breakdown of traditional life. These are all gateways into the central mountain, however it is named, and teaching any of those pathways is the essential work. Helping anyone move along one of those pathways, perhaps first as an intellectual analysis but eventually tapping deeper self-understanding, is participating in the great work. Each topic is connected by a thousand slender filaments to all the others. Pointing those out to the students is powerful teaching, which can release their own energies and desire to participate. Everyone who reads or hears this and every student in your classes will pick up the piece that speaks to her, and she will make it her own. This will ripple out into places you know nothing of. You can trust it will spread as it ought, and you can trust it will reach those ready to receive and live with it. It is an unusual text most of all because it can reach people on many different levels. Very few will grasp it all, but even fewer will receive nothing from it. The text will carry its own package of energy with it, which will facilitate its travels out into the world. You are merely its midwife. You are not responsible for its reception; that is our task.

This is all. Thank you.

Afterword

I had arrived at my island cabin in Lake Superior exhausted and full of grief over the world. The United States had once again invaded a country on false pretenses, for there were no weapons of mass destruction in Iraq; the images of the destruction and carnage were unbearable. I had just finished teaching a seminar on radical ecology, discussing the terrifying data about human impacts on our environment and what it would take to begin to reverse the catastrophic damage to the planet. Morning after morning I sat with my journal and poured out my anger and grief at a world that seemed to be spinning out into unknown territory. I wrote and wrote, hoping, I suppose, to drain out the frustration and heartache so I could fully arrive at my precious island retreat. It wasn't working. I couldn't extricate myself from the guilt of being a citizen of a powerful and dangerous country, and I was stunned by my hopelessness.

One morning as I wrote, a calm, confident voice said, "That's not how we see it." Really? What was that voice, and where did it come from? Shaken, I got up and took a walk. Something deep was astir. When I returned to my journal, only partly receptive to more surprises, I heard some more. It was a courteous offer of an extended explanation of why that mysterious voice understood the state of the earth so differently. Profoundly curious, I agreed immediately. I scribbled furiously, trying to catch every idea, pouring out step by logical step. In an hour I was exhausted. More came, morning after morning. After several days, I discovered I could write directly on my computer, which eased the process considerably.

This book is the result. In it, the mysterious voice, Manjushri, lays out an astonishing and challenging picture of our world at this moment. He describes a great shift of energy reaching the planet, "a shower of Spirit," to which we all are responding—some with new insights and wider consciousness and some with deep fear and violence. The problems that concern so many of us—environmental degradation, intense violent conflicts around the world, and the erosion of basic human stability and well-being in the face of modernization—are reframed as signs of profound opportunities for increased consciousness, recognition of systemic interdependence among all species, and exploration of how to be much more fully human. His understanding of what is possible now, in fact, what is already well underway, is grounded in a radical analysis of the implications of individualism and the rule of the ego, the penetration of markets into contemporary institutions and practices, the pervasive hegemony of science and materialism, and the destructive forces of globalization.

Readers who have studied this text have urged me to tell new readers to read it in small bits, a few pages at a time. I agree. Manjushri's analysis is so rich and at the same time so concise, it invites rereading and conversation. Instruction is certainly one of its purposes. Even more, the text intends to encourage us, especially those of us angry or grieving over the immense problems facing our world. For if we are encouraged, we will be able to create the change we so desperately need, to discover our full humanity.

Acknowledgments

I bow in gratitude to so many. These teachings appear now as a book because of the enthusiastic encouragement of its many readers around the world—from western Massachusetts to Bhutan, Great Britain, Italy, and Norway. Carol Drexler first explained to me I was channeling and has supported the project ever since. Jim Perkins first sent it out into the world, sharing it with his friends and organizing my first public talk. Don O'Shea, dean of faculty at Mount Holyoke College, insisted it have its own website and encouraged its publication. Eva Hooker shared her poetic and editorial expertise. Louise Cochran, Joan Davis, Jeana Edmonds, Paula Green, Olivia Hoblitzelle, Julia Jean, Randy Kehler, Shelton Maddox, Christian McEwen, Jorunn Ostberg, Lama Rangbar, Unni Snaprud, and Tom Wolff all offered suggestions and encouragement. To all, named and unnamed, my deepest gratitude for gently pushing the text and me out into the world.

CPSIA information can be obtained at www.ICGtesting.com
Printed in the USA
LVOW11s2325250215

428350LV00003B/9/P